455

D0045100

Limericks Historical and Hysterical

Limericks
Historical and
Hysterical

Plagiarized, Arranged, Annotated,
and Some Written by

Ray Allen Billington

SENIOR RESEARCH ASSOCIATE, THE HUNTINGTON LIBRARY

PH.D., (M.A. OXON), LITT.D., L.H.D., LL.D.

W. W. Norton & Company

NEW YORK / LONDON

Copyright © 1981 by W. W. Norton & Company, Inc.

Published simultaneously in Canada by George J. McLeod Limited, Toronto.

Printed in the United States of America

All Rights Reserved / First Edition

Library of Congress Cataloging in Publication Data

Billington, Ray Allen, 1903–

Limericks, historical and hysterical.

Bibliography: p.

Includes index.

1. Limericks.   I. Title.

PN6231.L5B47   811'.07   80–27951

ISBN 0–393–01453–3

W. W. Norton & Company, Inc. 500 Fifth Avenue, New York, N.Y. 10110

W. W. Norton & Company Ltd. 25 New Street Square, London EC4A 3NT

1 2 3 4 5 6 7 8 9 0

DEDICATED

TO THE MEMBERS OF

THE SOCIETY OF

THE FIFTH LINE

Whose Selfless Efforts to Preserve and Honor

a Unique Literary Form Deserve the Plaudits of

All True Friends of the Limerick

A C K N O W L E D G M E N T S

I am grateful to the learned permanent secretary pro tem

of the Society of the Fifth Line of Chicago and to

the members of that illustrious organization for permission

to reprint a number of examples of their creative genius,

to Playboy Enterprises Inc. for allowing me to use

selected verses from Playboy's Book of Limericks, *and*

to the editor of that fine publication, Clifford M.

Crist, who has aided me in various ways with his

unsurpassed knowledge of limerick lore. I am indebted,

too, to George P. Brockway, chairman of W. W. Norton

& Company, for suggesting this book. Its compilation

has afforded me more pleasure than writing any of

the historical works that are my usual medium.

—R A B

Contents

Limericks Historical and Hysterical

The Limerick and I[1]

$\mathscr{L}$et there be no misunderstanding. I am not a lyrical poet, not a gifted versifier, not even a competent composer of doggerel. By training, inclination, and profession I am an academician, a stodgy historian who has spent a lifetime writing learned (so-called) monographs in leaden prose, or preparing footnote-burdened articles for other historians to read. Mine is not the ability to sing in golden stanzas that will send spirits (and sometimes portions of the male anatomy) soaring. Seemingly nothing could be more remote from my interests or talents than that most challenging of all verse forms: the limerick.

Yet the limerick and I have enjoyed a happy love affair for half a century. Its beginning can be specifically dated. The year 1931 was one of excessive strain and tension: that spring I finally passed the qualifying examinations for a Harvard doctoral degree after months of terrifying apprehension; that summer I suffered a constant butterflies-in-the-stomach fear as I thought of facing my first teaching assignment that fall; that winter I lived under the threat that my temporary instructorship would not be renewed, and that I would be released into a depression-deflated job

---

[1] So strong is the habit among historians that I have even plagiarized the title to this introduction, slightly altering that of an autobiographical article that I was asked to write for the *Western Historical Quarterly,* 1 (January, 1970):5–20. This was called "The Frontier and I," and described my love affair with frontier history, which has been only slightly more passionate than that with the limerick.

market on the eve of the birth of my first child.[2] I could survive the ordeal, I thought, only if I could escape the real world into a land of fantasy.

That I found that outlet in the study of the limerick was linked to the doctoral dissertation that was under way at that time. A lean and frugal style, my Harvard professors told me, was the essence of good historical writing. As a former newspaper reporter, paid at space rates, I was inclined to excessive verbosity. I should practice some form of writing that forced me to compact large concepts into a minimum number of lines. What better medium for such an exercise than the limerick?[3]

That assignment led me into a good many hours of pleasant adventuring with words. It also resulted in several examples of the art form that have since found their way into published collections:

> There was a young man from Racine
> Who was weaned at the age of sixteen.
> He said, "I'll admit

---

[2] One faculty wife of mature years, looking back on that era of what academicians call "scholastic impotence" on the part of her graduate-school husband, has been generous enough to agree that the sacrifice was worthwhile:

> A scholar's old wife now recalls
> A life of limp prick and flat balls.
> But her mate's fertile pate,
> She is proud to relate,
> Spawned books that now cover their walls.

[3] For a time I was sufficiently audacious to flirt with the idea of attempting triolets, but soon abandoned that insanity. Thus I was less bold than the following heroine:

> A peculiar young poetess, Violet,
> Every day in her bath wrote a triolet.
> "Some compose," said she, "best
> When lying at rest,
> But I do my best work on the tiolet."

There's no milk in the tit,
But think of the fun it has been."[4]

There was a young man from Beirut
Who played penes as one might a flute,
    Till he met a sad eunuch
    Who lifted his tunic
And said, "Sir, my instrument's mute."[5]

A sly eunuch who lived in Port Said
Had a jolly good time while in bed,
    Nor could any sultana
    Detect from his manner
That he used a banana instead.

An old Jewish prophet named Moses,
Said: "A girl is a fool who supposes
    That a man, as a rule,
    Can boast of a tool
Proportionately long as his nose is."[6]

That taste of the verse form was sufficient to stir an
interest that persisted over the next quarter century. Not

---

[4] This effort is obviously faulted by the middle couplet, which is only slightly
altered from that in the well-known classic:
> There was an old lecher named Dave
> Who kept a dead whore in a cave.
>   He said: "I'll admit
>   I'm a bit of a shit,
> But think of the money I save."

[5] Honesty forces me to confess that this excellent verse and the two that follow
were the product of my talented wife's genius. Two of these have been immortalized
by inclusion in that bible of all limericists, Gershon Legman, *The Limerick* (Paris
1953), Nos. 1143 and 1321, as well as in other anthologies.

[6] An old wives' tale, now seriously questioned by the researches of Kinsey, Mas-
ters and Johnson, *et al.*, is that a young man's nose indicated the size of his penis.
Many a young lady who believed this tale was disappointed on her wedding night.

in writing limericks, for I was much too busy writing history to squander time on any nonessential scribbling, but in collecting. What a delightful hobby that proved to be. I soon compiled a respectable body of the hard-core classics, then began venturing into the byways of those more recently composed or less well known. Each new one was a treasured find. Some came from friends who learned of my interest; what a thrill to receive a note from a professor at Brown University with the enclosure:

> The wife of a chronic crusader
> Reproduced every courtier who laid her,
>> The amorous itch
>> Of this profligate bitch
> So dismayed the crusader, he spayed her.

Or to have a traveling publishers' representative (a breed famed for carrying gossip and bawdy stories from department to department) drop into my office with:

> From the depth of the crypt of St. Giles
> Came screams that reechoed for miles;
>> "Oh, my goodness gracious,"
>> Said Brother Ignatius,
> "I forgot that your Grace had the piles."

Thus my collection grew, page after page, until I had gathered a thousand or more,[7] all available at tongue tip to en-

---

[7] In this pursuit I was following the good example of another academician:
> There once was a young Ph.D.
> Who didn't like real poetry,
>> But only the kind
>> That began with the line:
> "There was a young girl et-c."

liven faculty parties or break the ice at more somber af-
fairs.

Then, in the early 1950s, a tragic blow fell on all lim-
erick collectors with the publication of Gershon Legman's
The Limerick: 1700 Examples with Notes, Variants and Index.
This noteworthy volume, we soon learned, was available
only in France, for the law mistakingly defined five-liners
as pornography in that less enlightened day, but I man-
aged to smuggle back a copy after a visit to Paris. As I
turned the pages my heart sank. They were all there—
every one that I had painfully collected over the years—
and a good many more besides. All carefully arranged,
with variants and alternate readings, dated as exactly as
possible, and bristling with the footnotes, appendices, and
other learned apparatus so dear to the hearts of academi-
cians. Gershon Legman, damn him, had compiled such a
definitive collection that collecting was no longer fun.

The limerick could still be enjoyed, obviously, only if
new examples of that illusive verse form were created. For-
tunately, I was living near Chicago at that time, where, I
was told, there existed a remarkable organization known as
the Society of the Fifth Line. Its members were scholars of
the utmost capacity, as familiar with ever variant in the lim-
erick form as Shakespeareans were with the bard's sonnets,
all of them masters of creativity who must produce an orig-
inal verse for each annual meeting of the membership.
Happily, I was deemed worthy of this elite society and each
year returned from its gatherings well laden with drink,
food, and a supply of fresh limericks that would satisfy my
cravings for another year. More of the Society of the Fifth
Line later in this book.

This was helpful, but not enough. The only way to sa-
tiate my lust for fresh material was to turn once more to
writing original limericks, some to be shared with my

brethren of the Fifth Line, some to be added to the neglected pages of my collection. I have continued that activity in a modest fashion ever since, with results hardly acceptable to purists, but providing me with a degree of satisfaction. In doing so, I have found three techniques helpful to the amateur.

One is to convert a current anecdote into the classic five-line form. A few years ago one such story came to my attention: a tale of a young man who, on his first date with a girl, asked if he might pull out a few hairs. "Why," she asked? "Because," said the swain, "I am collecting box tops." A minimum effort was needed to convert that into:

> There was a young fellow named Hector
> Who said to a girl as he necked her,
>   "Do you very much care
>   If I pull out some hair?
> You see, I'm a box-top collector."

An equally useful device as an aid to creativity is to dream up some new form of perversion or sexual gratification—admittedly not an easy assignment considering the time and talent devoted to that pursuit over the past centuries. But one can try and occasionally succeed:

> Said a zoo keeper's wife named Mallot,
> As she stuffed live ants up her twat,
>   "Of all sexual sensations,
>   The eccentric gyrations
> Of an anteater's tongue beats the lot."[8]

[8] One of my greatest ambitions was achieved in 1970 when the Society of the Fifth Line awarded this limerick the Duchess' Cup as the best (or worst) of the year. In all candor, it must also be reported that hearty dissent was voiced by one member of the jury on the grounds that we never learn whether the anteater consumed them all.

Experience taught me, finally, that if I allowed my
mind to roam freely in moments of relaxation, the subcon-
scious would sometimes produce useful inspiration. One
such moment occurred some years ago when I was
dragged to a recital. Listening to a contralto voice is a form
of agony that I compare unfavorably to a night in a medi-
eval torture chamber. As she sang of "Rose," "Rose," "Rose
all," "Rose all," my mind wandered. "Rose all . . . disposal
. . . sex with a disposal . . ." This was the result:

> Said a hardened old lecher named Mosul,
> In rejecting a young whore's proposal,
> > "I've so calloused my drill
> > That I can't get a thrill,
> Save by screwing a kitchen disposal."

This effort paid off well, for I was inspired to apply other
gadgets and modern inventions to the challenge of the lim-
erick form. Some of the results appear in the last chapter
of this book.

For a time these exercises in creativity satisfied my
taste for the exotic; but, alas, in recent years the thrill has
begun to fade. For this I can blame the revolution in stand-
ards of morality of the past few decades. Every proper lim-
erick, of course, must be improper. As a forgotten genius
of the form wrote many years ago:

> The limerick packs laughs anatomical
> Into space that is quite economical.
> > But the good ones I've seen
> > So seldom are clean,
> And the clean ones so seldom are comical.

So long as one could combine a sense of creativity with a
defiance of authority, limerick writing packed a double

thrill. Too, no one could be accused of crass materialism, for no respectable publisher would sully his good name with verse of such questionable morality. As one once testified:

> Said a printer well known for his wit,
> "There are certain bad words we omit.
>   It would sully our art
>   To print the word f---
> And we never, no never, use s---."

In those happy days, every limerick was an exercise in behind-the-barn adventuring, and therein lay its appeal.

But, alas, the sexual upheaval of the past decades has brought the five-liner out of the closet and into the book stall. No word is too unclean to be treasured in the privacy of one's own mind and collection. As one of venerable years I can sympathize with the anonymous poet who wrote:

> There was an old man from Freehold
> Who said, "The young, I am told,
>   Are so used to the nude
>   They don't think it lewd.
> My god, it is good to be old."

Fortunately, this revolution in moral standards has its positive side. The limerick has traditionally been the plaything of Oxford dons, American academicians, and a sprinkling of men of wit on both sides of the Atlantic. No longer. Today an art form long suppressed, or too long appreciated only by the few, has been made available to the many. The limerick has been democratized until it is within the reach of all. This transition can be stated in the traditional five lines:

> Time was when the limerick was fun;
> 'Twas a verse form all printers must shun.
>> But it's now so respectable,
>> It's even acceptable
> To W. W. Norton & Son.[9]

Taking advantage of this somewhat mixed blessing, I have dared make my slight contribution to an art form that may wither in the future under the bright light of acceptability. In doing so, I have been compelled to inflict my academic standards in an area where art should reign, using chapter headings, explanations, some variant readings, and such footnotes as needed to make the page unattractive. Habits are too strong to be broken, even when we realize that the footnote repels more than it attracts, and reveals more than most of us would like, particularly when it uses (as most must) that insipid *ibid.*:

> A wonderful word is the *ibid.*
> Its appearance is pale and insipid.
>> It stands as a sage
>> At the foot of the page,
> To tell whence the passage was cribbed.

The compulsions of scholarship have also compelled me to arrange the materials of this book by chapters, more or less governed by my own interests. The first deals with

---

[9]Of course anyone who glances at the title page of this book will realize that the correct name is "W. W. Norton & Co." But have you ever tried to rhyme "& Co."?

the historical uses of the limerick and is divided into two parts, one attempting to rescue from oblivion the American frontier that I have studied for a half century, the other dealing with World War II. I have included the latter largely because that event occurred during the height of my own collecting days, allowing me to parade materials little known to experienced collectors. Or so I hope.

A second section has been assembled from the files of the Society of the Fifth Line. Some of these have already found their way into anthologies, but more are little known and worthy of greater attention than they receive in the very limited publications of the society.

The third chapter brings together examples of the classic limerick form, some that I have written, some that friends have contributed, and more culled from collections both published and unpublished.

Finally, I am conscious of the limerick in its role as a mirror of social change. Authors have advanced perceptive opinions on a variety of current events, ranging from the conquest of space to modern styles. Here is grist for the historians of the future, and should be preserved. Examples in the last section, some borrowed from other collections, some written for the occasion, some adapted from the archives of the Society of the Fifth Line, are offered to those chroniclers who seek clues to an understanding of modern society in Britain and the United States.

Despite the elevated principles and educational ambitions that have motivated me as I have assembled this collection, I must confess that the task has been pleasureful. So much so that I have—in common with other collectors with a similar burning zeal—neglected my family connections. So the last line must, as usual, be written by our wives:

The limerick's a queer aberration.
It's a form of sex sublimation.
　　Words sent to the mind,
　　Like a "a rosy behind,"
End in doggerel, not copulation.

R.A.B.

CHAPTER I

Westward the Limerick

$\mathscr{F}$or reasons inexplicable, and quite unpredictable (limerick writing does get in one's blood) fifth liners have paid but scant attention to the American West. This is surprising. Novelists, film makers, and television producers have all found the big sky country an irresistible (and commercially successful) setting for their dramas. They have elevated the cowboy to the pinnacle of the pantheon of folk heroes; that Galahad of the plains has been riding hell for leather across book pages and silver screens for almost a century, with no sign that his popularity will ever wane. Yet not a single collection or anthology contains a limerick about cowboys.[1] Or, for that matter, miners or ranchers or prospectors or any other of the galaxy of heroes who subdued the wild frontier.

Why this alarming gap in our cultural heritage? Timid beginners among limerick writers might point out the difficulty of rhyming many of the words that we associate with

[1] One of the very few exceptions is a limerick that obviously uses the word "cowboy" to provide a needed meter, not because his occupation was essential to the theme.

> An amorous cowboy from Rio
> Once met a young lady named Cleo.
>   A full night and a day
>   They spent in the hay,
> And now the poor cowboy can't pee-o.

the frontier. Who, for example, could knowingly match a first line that ended with "Navajo,"[2] "Apache," "Comanche," "Grosventre," "Assiniboin," "San Jacinto," "Lapwai," "Klamath," "Ezekiel Williams," or "Nuestra Padre San Francisco de los Tejas?" What experienced versifier could construct a properly metered line built about such words as "Opechancanough," "Tlacatecuhtli," "Tenochtitlán," or "Huitzilopochtle"? The challenge, indeed, is formidable.

That this deterrent has slowed the writing of limericks is suggested by the fact that the one Indian tribe to be glorified in a number of fifth liners is the Sioux. Thus:

> There once was a sensuous Sioux
> Who liked to do nothing but scrioux;
>   She would give no relief
>   To her favorite chief,
> Until both of his balls turned blioux.

In such classics the appeal, obviously, was to capitalize on the opportunity for eccentric spelling variations invited by "ew"/"ioux" possibilities, not the record of a great Indian nation.

The paucity of western limericks cannot, however, be explained solely by linguistic complications. Purists might shy from using "Geronimo" or "Tonopah" because of problems of rhyme or meter, but other names associated with the frontier offered no such excuse. "Dodge City," for example, offers a tempting field to rhymsters; so do Monterey and Santa Fe and Montana and dozens more. Yet

---

[2] One of the delights of limerick scholarship is the creativity that such efforts inspire. When I complained to a friend the difficulty of rhyming "Navajo" he emerged after a weekend of labor with the passable verse that appears later in this chapter.

they have been ignored, while such a distant spot as Bombay, in far off India, has produced a variety of characters male and female; the males are famed for fashioning a cunt out of clay, jerking themselves off in a sleigh, diddling a girl in a sleigh, buggering their father one day, and thinking that syphilis just went away; the ladies for never thinking themselves gay and being put in a family way. The list could be expanded, but the point is clear. The American West has been shamefully neglected by purveyors of a significant portion of our cultural heritage.

The pages that follow offer a feeble attempt to remedy this deficiency and add the limerick to the other media that glorify America's frontier background. Admittedly, many of the rhymes are farfetched; admittedly the meter is strained now and then. These defects can be ascribed partly to the fact that I have been forced to write a good many myself, partly due to the necessity of including any classic dealing with the West, even though marred by imperfections. As a historian of the frontier, I insist that it be properly represented in this book, even if in imperfect rhetoric.

Included in this section, too, is a sampling of limericks written during World War II. These limericks are included partly because I was collecting avidly during the war years, and need only to turn to the notebooks kept at that time for a usable supply. Many deserve to be remembered, moreover, for the light that they shed on the nation's problems and mood amid a conflict that required every sacrifice for victory. Others mirror the deep-seated antagonisms bred of a struggle for survival against Nazis, Facists, and Japanese militants.

The usability of a limerick as an educational device can be well illustrated by this little-known classic:

Said a greedy old whore from Willamette,
As she ran the army camp gamut,
    "I could make a lot more
    But I'm only one whore.
I feel like a bottleneck, damn it."[3]

What better device than this verse to bring home to today's youth the agonizing days just after America's entry into the war, when its industrial capacity was strained to the utmost, and where the "bottlenecks" that developed in industry after industry slowed production. That phrase played a prominent role in the nation's vocabulary during those years.

    May the limericks that follow play a role in perpetuating the memory of America's pioneer days when women and the West were wild, and may they enlighten today's generation on the problems of whoring amidst wartime's terrors.

Amarillo

A cowgirl from old Amarillo
Kept finding strange heads on her pillow.
    She decided one day
    To keep them away
By stuffing her sweet parts with Brillo.

Armadillo

While Sue lay supine 'neath a willow,
She was screwed by a large armadillo,

---

[3] This limerick is doubly instructive, for it tells us about the "bottlenecks" that plagued industry during the early months of World War II, and teaches us the correct pronunciation of the Oregon valley where the Reverend Jason Lee established his famous Indian mission in 1834.

And remarked to the same,
As both of them came,
That the next time he might bring a pillow.

Old trappers were oft heard to say   *Beaver*
The beaver was not a bad lay.
    But buggery ain't easy
    For the timid or queasy,
For the tail always gets in the way.

When a lady returned from Big Moose,   *Big Moose*
Her husband exclaimed, "What the deuce,
    I'm quite reconciled
    To the call of the wild,
But where did you get the papoose?"

There was a young lady from Tryson   *Bison*
Who conceived mad love for a bison.
    After love's fruition
    Her snatch's condition
Was never again so enticing.[4]

There was a young lady from Butte   *Butte*
Who said to her husband, "You brute,
    Your nasty old sassage
    Has stunk up my passage.
From now on I'm sticking to fruit.

[4]Presumably the possibility of a permanently enlarged snatch did not occur to the character in a well-known verse:
> A habit obscene and bizarre
> Has taken a hold on papa.
>   He brings home camels
>   And other large mammals
> And gives them a go at mama.

Calamity Jane

'Twas said that Calamity Jane
Found women and men both a pain.
So when in her nightie
This hermaphrodit-e
Fucked herself—which is hard to explain.

Cheyenne

Said a full-blooded northern Cheyenne,
After tryin' and tryin' and tryin',
"Enough is enough.
An unfillable muff
Is no place for a Cheyenne to die in."

Cowboy

A cowboy when filled with strong beer
Loved to roger his horse from the rear.
When asked if he'd care
If it wasn't a mare,
Said: "Of course I would care; I'm not queer."

Cowboy

A hardened old cowboy named Buck
With women just never had luck.
They'd kiss and they'd squeeze,
And his pecker they'd tease,
But he never could get them to fuck.

Custer

When Custer was resting at ease,
Which was between massacrees,
He would lie around bare
With his dong in the air,
Which he cooled in the soft evening breeze.[5]

[5] Colonel Custer has inspired at least one other limerick, which is weakened when it elevates him to a generalship, a rank that he held only briefly and then as a brevet general:

When General George A. Custer
Was full of fire and bluster,
He'd grab a young Sioux
And run her right through
With his big, pink personal thruster.

An Indian, who claims we can trust her,   *Custer*
Insists she was raped by George Custer.
    Despite what he planned,
    His three-inch last stand,
Was all Colonel Custer could muster.

While awaiting the Sioux to disband,   *Custer*
Colonel Custer took matters in hand.
    Despite his dejection
    He achieved an erection.
That was *almost* Custer's Last Stand.

There's a Texan oil driller named Fells,   *Dallas*
And sad is the story he tells:
    "I've drilled cunt with my phallus
    From Lubbock to Dallas,
And all that I find are dry wells."

There was an old whore from Des Moines   *Des Moines*
Who would take any man 'tween her loins;
    All she asked from each mate
    Was a very small rate,
Like a nickle, or other small coins.[6]

Cowboys at the end of the drive   *Dodge City*
Were so horny they scarce could survive.
    So the whores of Dodge City
    Out of greed (not of pity)
Worked double shifts: nine until five.

---

[6] Her habits, clearly, were the opposite of those of another lady of pleasure probably employed in the same house:
> There was an old whore from Des Moines
> Who had a large sack full of coins.
>   The nickles and dimes
>   She got from the times
> She admitted the boys to her loins.

Dodge City	In story and film old Dodge City Was a center for sex and tough titty. 　　But historians have shown 　　That image overblown. It was moral and quiet (a pity).[7]
Durango	A virgin who came from Durango Always diddled herself with a mango. 　　"It's delightful," she said, 　　"To lie on the bed, And put it where I won't let a man go."
Gun slingers	The gun, the head shrinkers tell us, Is man's substitute for a phallus, 　　So the western gun slingers, 　　Having tiny whing-dingers, Made corpses, not girls, for their solace.
Helena	A drunken old miner from Helena Was walking one night when he fell in a 　　Prospector's ditch. 　　No, he didn't get rich. What he said was so bad I'm not tellin' ya.
Hickok	As a gunslinger Wild Bill Hickok Had mastered every known trick-shot. 　　But his skills while in bed 　　Leave less to be said, For nothing could make his small dick hot.

---

[7] The sad fact is that in all the cattle towns, including Dodge City, only forty-five men were killed (including sixteen by police) and of these thirty-nine died of gun-shot wounds, not six-shooters. These unglamorous facts are revealed in a romance-shattering volume by Robert R. Dykstra, *The Cattle Towns* (New York, 1968). So much for the walk-down and the shoot-out.

Said a girl who came west to a farm,   *Kansas*
"City life has a far greater charm.
    Take the pleasures of orgasm—
    Each urban girl has 'em,
But in Kansas they're viewed with alarm."

There was a young lady named Knox   *Knox*
Who diddled herself with large rocks.
    So hot was her tail,
    When she used western shale,
Oil spurted in jets from her box.

The explorers Lewis and Clark   *Lewis and Clark*
Found their expedition a lark,
    For Sacagawea,
    Let both of them lay 'er—
That discovery they kept in the dark.[8]

Said the ring-tailed roarer, Mike Fink,   *Mike Fink*
"Be warned that when I'm in the pink,
    I'll outgouge and outbite
    Any raftsman who might
Reveal that I have a small dink."[9]

---

[8] This is an obvious canard conceived by a desperate limerick writer. Actually Sacagawea, the Shoshoni who served an invaluable role as interpreter and guide, was accompanied on the expedition by her loyal husband, Toussaint Charbonneau, and their eight-week-old baby. Any doubter has only to look in Ella E. Clark and Margaret Edmonds, *Sacagawea of the Lewis and Clark Expedition* (Berkeley, 1980).

[9] That Mike Fink, the legendary hero of the Mississippi River keelboatmen, may have been less than adequately endowed is suggested by the fact that all of the stories about him stress his abilities as a rough-and-tumble fighter, and not his prowess in bed. On the other hand, this reticence may have been a product of Victorian prudery rather than proof of a tiny pecker. Unfortunately, the standard work by Walter Blair and Franklin J. Meine, *Mike Fink: King of the Mississippi Keelboatmen* (New York, 1933), fails to come to grips with this problem.

Montana	Said a herder who watched o'er his band,
	"This Montana's a very strange land.
	So long as I'm frigid,
	My digit is rigid.
	Liking chinooks I don't understand."

Montana	A cowboy from eastern Montana
	Had a cock like a ten-inch banana.
	When he used this great prick,
	He had to come quick,
	Then to bring the girl to had to fan 'er.[10]

Montana	A cowboy who came from Montana
	Found sex in a devious manner.
	He bored monstrous holes
	In telegraph poles,
	And thrust in his giant banana.

Monterey	A *ranchero* in Old Monterey,
	Put his mares in a family way.
	His offspring thus sired,
	Were so widely admired,
	Their offspring run the state to this day.

Mountain Man	"I wonder," a Mountain Man said,
	"What fucking is like in a bed.
	I'm so used to tall grass

[10] In fairness to the cowboy, the girls that he screwed might have been prone to the fashionable faints common among nineteenth-century ladies. This is suggested by:

> There was a young lady named Anna,
> With a face like a purple bandanna.
> Screwed again and again
> She would faint from the strain,
> And the fellow on top had to fan 'er.

On my balls and my ass,
That I prefer the prairie instead."

A whore from the plains of Nebraska
Would do anything that you asked her.
　　You could lay her all day,
　　At nominal pay,
But, oh, how you paid nine days after.

Nebraska

A lady from west Oklahoma
Always came when she heard *La Paloma*.
　　But in Mexico City,
　　Ah! More is the pity,
The lady is still in a coma.

Oklahoma

There was a young lady in Reno,
Who lost all her dough playing keno.
　　But she lay on her back,
　　Exposing her crack,
And now she owns the casino.

Reno

Said a wench from Rio del Norte,
"I prefer to fuck men over forty.
　　It's always too quick
　　With a young fellow's prick;
I like it to last and be warty."

Rio del Norte

A young Mormon maid from Salt Lake
Liked to cock-tease boys on the make.
　　She was finally the prize
　　Of a man twice her size,
And all she recalls is the ache.

Salt Lake

San Juan
Capistrano
	The Mission San Juan Capistrano
	Lures swallows with all their guano.
	    The odorous turds
	    Of these wayfaring birds
	Spread smog from Del Mar to Oceano.[11]

Santa Fe	An old whore who worked Santa Fe
	Was known as a luscious hot lay.
	    But the bugs in her twitchet
	    Forced her always to itch it,
	And frightened her clients away.

Santa Fe	A cowboy from Old Santa Fe
	Seemed to women the ultimate lay.
	    His machismo was such
	    Girls swooned at his touch.
	But to tell you the truth, he was gay.[12]

Seattle	There was a young girl from Seattle,
	Who loved to be rogered by cattle,
	    'Til a bull from Montana
	    Attacked in a manner
	That made both her ovaries rattle."

[11] Del Mar, as any race-track fan knows, is just north of San Diego; Oceano is just south of Pismo Beach. And anyone who doesn't know where Pismo Beach is shouldn't admit his ignorance.

[12] The classic study of the homosexual cowboy is Clifford P. Westermeier, "Cowboy Sexuality: A Historical No-No?" *Red River Valley Historical Review,* 2 (Spring, 1975):93–113. This gifted author has contributed several limericks to bolster his arguments, including:

> There once was a cowboy named Hooter
> Who packed a gigantic six-shooter.
>   When he grabbed the large stock
>   It became hard as rock.
> As a "piece" maker it couldn't be cuter.

A well-hung young Oglala Sioux   *Sioux*
Told girls that he always withdrew.
    Those who believed
    Very often conceived.
'Twas too long to get out 'fore he blew.

There was an old squaw from the Sioux   *Sioux*
Who was screwing herself with a shoe.
    While enjoying the feel
    Of the sole and the heel,
The tongue was so ticklish, she blew.

A Comstock miner named Tutrow,   *Sutro*
With salves and massage made his root grow.
    It grew and it grew,
    'Til he only could screw
The tunnel of Adolph H. Sutro.[13]

With two bolts of the drink Taos Lightning[14]   *Taos*
Señoritas felt their labia tightening.
    The effect on the men
    Was the opposite, so when
They united, their passion was frightening.

---

[13] "Sutro's Tunnel," completed in 1878, penetrated four miles into Mount Davidson to tap the famed Comstock Lode in its lower reaches, allowing ventilation, drainage, and easy extraction of the ore. Obviously, the miner who used this vast hole for his sexual gratification was a well-hung man. Of him it could be said, as was said of the young man from Quebec who could put it right up to the neck: "My, he had a big one, didn't he?" For the insatiably curious the whole story is told in Robert E. and Mary F. Stewart, *Adolph Sutro, a Biography* (Berkeley, 1962), which for some reason fails to mention the miner named Tutrow.

[14] "Taos Lightning," a whiskey produced by several distillers in that New Mexican outpost and illegally but widely used in the Rocky Mountain fur trade, was generally believed to be concocted from raw alcohol, nitroglycerine, and equal parts of Tabasco sauce and tobacco juice.

Tool

When the white man attempted to rule,
The Indians made him a fool.
  They cut off his nuts
  To hang in their huts,
And stuffed up his mouth with his tool.

Tuckahoe

An Algonquin brave from Old Tuckahoe
At any old crack would have a go,
  But when he went west
  He sought only the best,
As found in the liveliest Navajo.

Utah

Brigham Young was never a neutah,
A pansy, or virgin, or fruitah.
  When fifty-three virgins
  Succumbed to his urgin's,
He founded the great state of Utah.[15]

*Yellowstone
Basin*

When he entered the Yellowstone Basin
John Colter felt his pecker start raisin',
  For the sulphurous stench
  Brought to mind the Crow wench
And the sniff of the guiff he'd been chasin'.[16]

Yellowstone Park

The caldrons of Yellowstone Park
Are no place to have sex in the dark.
  A young ranger tried—

[15] While there is documentary proof of Brigham Young's "sealing" to fifty-three wives, historians estimate that the total was nearer seventy. That all of these were virgins is doubtful, for many were at an advanced age when "sealed," and sustained virginity on the frontier was rare. A list of all seventy is in Stanley P. Hirshson, *The Lion of the Lord: A Biography of Brigham Young* (New York, 1969), pp. 184–223.

[16] The author of this limerick has cunningly avoided a stand on the controversial question of whether John Colter, a famed trapper and Mountain Man of the early nineteenth century, actually discovered Yellowstone Park. The best evidence today suggests that he did not, although the region was known for years as "Colter's Hell."

Now his balls look deep-fried
And his prick like a stick sans its bark.

There was a young fellow from Yuma,   *Yuma*
Who essayed to bugger a puma,
    In the midst of his frolics
    It clawed off his bollicks,
Leaving both in a very bad humor.

And now, in defiance of all the laws of rhetoric that
demand a smooth-flowing transition, to a few reminders of
the era of World War II:

A female Nazi from Bredo   *Bredo*
Advances her sinister credo,
    By displaying her charms
    During air raid alarms,
Inflaming the warden's libido.

They say that Galeazzo Ciano[17]   *Ciano*
Plays Bach with his cock on the piano.
    If he does, it's the most
    Fascist culture can boast
In this day of dominae anno.

O soldiers come back to us clean!   *Clean*
Wear rubbers—you know what I mean.
    Though I'd very much ruther

[17]Happily, the world has forgotten Galeazzo Ciano, who was foreign minister
under Mussolini, and responsible for the ravage of Ethiopia.

You'd bugger each other
Than any French whore that I've seen.

Der Führer

When Der Führer had ended life's lot,
He stormed St. Pete's gate on the dot:
        "Let me in, I'm no kike,
        I'm head man of the Reich."
Christ shrugged and replied: "Vell, so vot?"

Ed

There was a young monarch named Ed,
Who took Mrs. Simpson to bed.
        As they bounced up and down,
        He said: "Bother the crown,
Let them give it to Georgie instead."[18]

ETUSA

When a young man out on ETUSA[19]
Sees a girl he probably screws her.
        He pops in and out
        While marching about
To the tunes of John Philip Sousa.

France

An oversexed GI in France
Decided to take just a chance,
        But the fairest of fox holes
        In Paris are pox holes,
And now he's got France in his pants.

---

[18] The heroic sacrifice of King Edward VIII has never been properly celebrated
by limerick makers. A monarch who placed screwing above ruling in his scale of
values deserves their enthusiastic applause. Edward renounced his throne to marry
Mrs. Wallis Warfield Simpson in June, 1937, after the British government refused
to allow his marriage as king to a divorced woman. His brother, George VI, as-
cended the throne.

[19] Those with inadequate memories will be panting to know that these initials
stand for European Theater, United States of America, and were widely used dur-
ing the war.

There was an old Jew from the ghetto,   *Ghetto*
Who fearlessly wrote a libretto,
    Calling Hitler a slitch,
    A bastard, a bitch.
But he sang it in whispered falsetto.[20]

When a Lieutenant Colonel named Bobby   *Hobby*
Announced that his privates were nobby,
    Ten thousand young WACS
    Fell flat on their backs
And cried, as they avidly opened their cracks,
"To hell with Oveta Culp Hobby."[21]

'Twas said by Madam Lupescu,   *Lupescu*
Who came to Roumania's rescue,
    "It's a very nice thing
    To be under a king.
Is democracy better? I esk you."[22]

A lady of doubtful nativity   *Nativity*
Had an ass of extreme sensitivity;
    She could sit on the lap
    Of a Nazi or Jap,
And detect Fifth Column activity.

[20] Another view of the Nazi-Jewish relationship is suggested by:
    There was a young Nazi amoeba,
    Fell in love with a Jewess named Reba.
      The primeval jelly,
      Would crawl 'crost her belly,
    And gently whisper, "Ich liebe."

[21] Should anyone be interested, Oveta Culp Hobby became director of the Woman's Army Auxiliary Corps when it was formed in 1942 and served until 1945. This verse must have been written early in the war, for not ten thousand but a hundred thousand WACS had enlisted by the end of the conflict. Or perhaps ninety thousand of them were lesbians.

[22] Those with memories as short as mine will need to be reminded that in December, 1925, Prince Carol of Roumania renounced the right to succession to the throne, preferring to live in exile with his mistress, Magda Lupescu. Cheers to him.

Peking

A slant-eyed young girl from Peking
Said of the Rape of Nanking,
    "Every Jap in North China
    Has explored my vagina;
It's so sore I can't pee through the thing."[23]

Ration

An Italian lady of fashion,
When e'er she was swept by a passion,
    Would leap into bed
    With a leer as she said,
"Here's one thing Il Duce can't ration."[24]

Seamen

There was a young lady from Beaman,
Who was known as a sexual demon.
    "These soldiers," said she,
    "Mean nothing to me,
For what I like is the seamen."

Sparse

While praise for a sitzkrieg is sparse,
To lose one approaches a farce.
    Yet the pain of defeat,
    Isn't rendered more sweet,
By being a pain in the arse.[25]

USO

In the army and navy the toast is
To the talented USO hostess

[23] No, Nanking was not a girl, but the Chinese city that fell to the Japanese invaders in December, 1937.

[24] This version seems to have been the first of a limerick that has appeared in several anthologies as:

> There was a young lady of fashion
> With oodles and oodles of passion.
>   To her lover, she said,
>   As they climbed into bed,
> "Here's one thing the bastards can't ration."

[25] When Nazi forces regrouped after their "blitzkrieg" of Poland, their delay was derisively labeled a "sitzkrieg" by limerick makers. Alas, they gloated too soon.

Who was diddled and screwed
While she tried to conclude
Which service she really liked mostest.

Don't dip your prick in a WAC.   *WAC*
Don't ride the breast of a WAVE.
    Just sit in the sand
    And do it by hand
And buy bonds with the money you save.[26]

There was an old madam in Sfax   *WACS*
Whose morals were frightfully lax.
    She'd not only cohabit
    More ways than a rabbit,
But tutored young WACs in her knacks.

Shed a tear for a WAVE named McGinnis,   *WAVE*
To whose naval career was writ finis.
    She did not understand
    The boswain's command,
To break out the admiral's pinnace.

A WAVE who had duty at sea,   *WAVE*
Complained that it hurt her to pee.
    Said the Chief Bosun's mate,
    "That accounts for the fate
Of the cook and the captain and me."[27]

---

[26] This verse, although faulty in rhyme and meter, is included to illustrate the
distortions that excessive patriotism could produce among limerick makers.

[27] Motivated, no doubt, by the highest nationalistic interests, the concocter of
this limerick simply adapted a venerable version that had been known since the
1920s:

> There was a young lady at sea
> Who said: "God, how it hurts me to pee."
>   Said the brawny old mate,
>   "That accounts for the fate
> Of the captain, the purser, and me."

CHAPTER II

Gems from the Society of the Fifth Line

The Society of the Fifth Line
Meets yearly for food, wit, and wine.
The limericks recited
Make me feel benighted—
They're always much better than mine.

*L*imerick collectors throughout the world, from Tiburon to Timbuktu, owe a debt of gratitude to those masters of the medium who gather in Chicago each May to celebrate the annual meeting of the Society of the Fifth Line. These are the foremost perpetrators of an art form that has contributed immeasurably to the world's culture—and entertainment. From their meetings comes a fund of lore that inspires all aficionados; from them, too, comes a wealth of freshly conceived verses that bear the stamp of the genius of their creators.

The Society of the Fifth Line has been gathering yearly each May for almost thirty years. Its origins reach back to the early 1950s, when a few specialists, led by a prominent Chicago attorney who has ever since served as its secretary pro tem, decided to exchange enthusiasm and verses from their collections in a properly convivial setting.

Its chronology since that time is difficult to trace. According to the secretary's minutes the thirty-first annual meeting was held in 1964, the seventy-fifth in 1966, the seventy-sixth and seventy-seventh in 1967, the seventy-eighth in both 1968 and 1969, and the two hundred first in 1977.

More sober analysis (something rarely found at the meetings) indicates that the society met first in 1953, for in that year and the next sizable collections of mimeographed materials were distributed to the members. In 1958 publication of the proceedings began, usually in a handsomely printed and bound limited edition (that for 1962, when the discussion centered about "The Gray Flannel Limerick; or, Friendly Persuasion through the Ages," appeared in a binding of gray flannel).

These meetings are models of wit and wisdom. Bountiful drink and savory foodstuffs provide energy for the informal formalities that follow: an exchange of current anecdotes (sometimes called dirty stories); a roll call in which each member must respond with a limerick new to the membership (impossible save when the verse is written especially for the occasion); a paper or two expertly examining some subject famed in limerick lore (one dwelt at length with the problem of buggering a squid); the singing of a verse or two from the official society hymn, "Cleft of Ages, Rock for Me"; and always the Norman Douglas Memorial Lecture, named in honor of the British scholar whose learned work, *Some Limericks,* is the bible of all true collectors.

The Norman Douglas Memorial Lecture is always the high point of the evening. The first, delivered in 1958, expertly explored a topic vital to all masters of limerickology: "Where the Scatological Is the Necessary: A Prolegomena of the Poetics of the Limerick." Those that followed have maintained the same high intellectual level as they roamed

48

from discussions of "Some Little Known Limericks of Ella Wheeler Wilcox" to "The Five Lines of Force of Gall and Spurzheim" and "The Curious Case of the Crypto-Limerick." Each has been enriched by a half-dozen limericks especially written to illuminate the subject under discussion. Each that is particularly favored by the discriminating audience is greeted with shouts of "Boo Lear, Boo Lear"—a dubious tribute to the Edward Lear who popularized the limerick form in the nineteenth century but committed the unpardonable sin of repeating the first line as the last.

One significant contribution of each meeting of the society is a fresh supply of verses to refresh the collections of aficionados throughout the world. Some are the product of a genius that Shakespeare or Milton or Edgar Guest might envy, created by members of the society over the past year. Or, more properly, allegedly created, for the origin of the materials that appear in its publications is not always known, due, probably, to the modesty of those who hide beneath the cloak of anonymity. Thus:

> There was a young preacher from China,
> Who loved boys but thought birds diviner.
> > But he gets little tail—
> > In fact he's in jail,
> Being charged with corrupting a mynah.

or:

> Lady Eva of East Birmingham
> Got caught in a terrible jam.
> > While out on a bust
> > She put too much trust
> In the fit of a friend's diaphragm.

Others reveal only slightly less evidence of the genius of their creators. Those that follow are representative of the hundreds in the archives of the society. They, and others that space limitations have excluded, deserve immortality.

Abbot

There once was an amorous abbot,
Who longed to get into the habit
    Of a virginal nun
    Whom he scragged on the run.
(They've injected her pee in a rabbit.)

Abstention

A matron who favored abstention,
Had breasts of unequal dimension.
    When woo'd by her hubby,
    She withheld the large bubby,
Creating domestic dissension.[1]

Alice

An hermaphrodite person named Alice
Could pick up loose coins with her phallus.
    But it could't make change,
    Which narrowed her range,
And kept her from playing the Palace.

Binger

There was a young German named Binger
Who was screwing an opera singer.

[1] The composer of that bit of verse probably had in mind the justly famed classic:

> Said the Duke to the Duchess of Beckwith,
> "Though foreshortened, of course, in perspective,
>   Has your east tit the least bit
>   The best of your west tit,
> Or is my eyesight defective?"

He said with delight,
"That's sure in there tight."
Said she: "You mean that's not just your finger?"

"We are ladies here at Sweet Briar,"   *Briar*
The dean told the girls. "We require
   That you peddle your ass,
   If you must, outside class,
And at all times in formal attire.

A postulant, perfect and celibate,   *Celibate*
Found his passions beginning to well a bit.
   But his nightly repression
   Found fluid expression
And annointed the roof of his cell a bit.

My sextagenarian chum,   *Chum*
Who's been fucking one broad in a slum
   For forty-four years,
   Will retire, he fears,
Before his old pecker can come.

A cabby's wife, brighter than some,   *Come*
Had a meter installed on her bum,
   With a musical chime
   To keep track of the time,
And allow you to pay as you come.[2]

[2] She was less kind than a well-known shady sister of hers:
   A harlot who practiced at Yale
   Had her price tattooed on her tail,
     And on her behind,
     To be kind to the blind,
   Was a special edition in Braille.

Conversion

At a born-again Baptist conversion,
A preacher kept urging a virgin,
    'Til she finally gave in,
    When he said: "It's no sin,
So long as it's total immersion."

Crete

A young ballerina from Crete
Offered stagehands all they could eat.
    When one asked for a ride,
    She regretfully sighed,
"That would ruin my nutcracker, sweet."

Druel

King Wenceslas's page, Master Druel,
Had no feast for Christmas, just gruel.
    "Like I told you for years,
    You should clean out your ears,
What I wanted was faggots, not fuel."

Experiment

Said a physics prof, "Girls, this experiment
Is mistakingly 'rousing your merriment.
    When I said, 'to stop stalls,
    Spin the governor's balls,'
My own weren't precisely the pair I meant."

Flock

After scolding his penitent flock,
The pontiff exhorted his cock:
    "You pendulous shrimp,
    You just dangle there limp,
You're supposed to be Peter, the Rock."

Ghent

There was a young lady from Ghent,
Who said she knew what it meant,
    When men asked her to dine,
    Fed her whiskey and wine.
She knew what it meant—but she went.

A free-lancing artist named Greeley,   *Greeley*
Had a model that suited ideally.
    At first scent of paint,
    She would fall in a faint,
And only revive when screwed freely.[3]

The thirteenth is the day of St. Jarlath,   *Jarlath*
A Norman who lithped when he parleth,
    Said he: "With a nun,
    I have sanctified fun,
Which would be mortal sin with a harloth."

An obese old broker named Kip   *Kip*
Took a very fat girl on a trip.
    He was talking of stock
    When he put in his cock.
At the end she said: "Thanks for the tip."

A lusty old man from Lahore   *Lahore*
Had a penis of six feet or more.
    You'd think he'd be glad,
    But instead he was sad;
He could use but the first three or four.[4]

---

[3] She was clearly less desirable than the model employed by Titian:
    While Titian stood mixing rose madder,
    His model posed nude on a ladder.
        Her position, to Titian,
        Suggested coition,
    So he leaped up the ladder, and had her.
[4] Equally unfortunate was his neighbor, whose complaint was the opposite:
    There was a young man from Lahore
    Whose prick was one inch and no more,
        It was all right for keyholes
        And little girls' pee holes,
    But not worth a damn with a whore,

Land   Moaned Tessie the whore: "In this land,
I've met bastards who thought it was grand
To retire, when inclined,
With sex problems in mind,
And awake with solution in hand."

Lapp   There was a young lecher named Lapp,
Who thought condoms were just so much crap.
Said he: "All us he-men
Like to scatter our semen."
Three weeks later he still has the clap.

Last   An emasculate lad said: "At last,
I've an elephant's trunk for a mast.
Though usually great,
I do have to state,
I'm embarrassed when peanuts are passed."

Leeds   A lecherous curate of Leeds
Was discovered one day in the weeds,
Astride a young nun.
He said: "Christ, this is fun,
Far better than telling one's beads."

Lent   A friar of peculiar intent
Gave up pederasty for Lent.
But just to make sure
His resolve remained pure,
He pounded a cork in his vent.[5]

[5] He was obviously following the example of two young ladies well known to limerick collectors:

> There was a young lady from Warwick
> Who tried to avoid the storick
> By preparing each day
> For the nocturnal lay
> By plugging her womb with a corick.

To her gardener a lady named Lilliom   *Lilliom*
Said: "Billy, plant roses and trillium."
    Then she started to fool
    With the gardener's tool,
And wound up in a bed of Sweet William.

Said a naval cadet named Lorenz,   *Lorenz*
"I've a terrible case of the bends.
    No, it's not from deep diving.
    It's the gobs who keep trying
To turn me to nautical ends."

Said his virginal bride to McNary,   *McNary*
"I've saved myself just for you, Harry."
    But to his chagrin,
    When he poked his way in,
He found there were seeds in the cherry.

There was a young lady from Maine   *Maine*
Who declared she'd a man on the brain.
    But you knew from the view
    Of the way her waist grew,
It was not on her brain he'd lain.[6]

Another young lady from Warwick
Plugged herself up with a corick.
    She explained: "It's less svelte
    Than a chastity belt
But more easily removed with a forick."

[6]Her fate was similar to that of another unwed mother:
There was a young lady from Thrace
Whose corsets grew too tight to lace.
    Her father said, "Nelly,
    There's more in your belly
Than ever got there through your face."

Medinah

Mohammed, when lodged in Medinah,
Imported a fifth wife from China,
 Being anxious to know
 If it really were so
That Chinese have a squinted vagina.[7]

Mither

Little Nellie, while still in her mither,
Would wiggle and gyrate and slither,
 To place her wee cunt
 Right up to the front,
So dad diddled the duo togither.

Moody

A warm-hearted William Vaughan Moody
Told every old bag that he screwed, he
 Charged nothing for fucks,
 Whether plain or deluxe,
"Shucks, mam, it's no more than my duty."[8]

Myrtle

A cute English lassie named Myrtle
Was so fecund and fruitful and fertile,
 She was got with a child
 By the gay Oscar Wilde,
Through a crack in her chastity girdle.[9]

---

[7] So universal was this misconception concerning the anatomy of Oriental women that the Chinese prostitutes of San Francisco in the gold-rush days used to call from their cribs: "Two-bitee lookee, four bitee feelee, six bitee doee," or so it has been said.

[8] There is no evidence that William Vaughan Moody, a prominent poet and play-wright of the late nineteenth century, ever uttered these noble words, but the fact that one of his best-known plays was called *The Great Divide* indicates that he was capable of sexual interests.

[9] That the art of limerick writing has progressed mightily is clear when we compare this lucid verse with one glorifying the same heroine but written in the 1920s:

> There was a young lady named Myrtle
> Who had an affair with a turtle.
> She had crabs, so they say,
> In a year and a day,
> Which proves that the turtle was fertile.

Said a history professor named Ned   *Ned*
To a redheaded co-ed in his bed,
   "The weather's too sultry,
   For committing adultery.
Won't you swallow my pride, dear, instead?"[10]

At a wedding reception when tight,   *Night*
Was an actress who'll murder on sight
   A depraved guest who cried
   To the virginal bride,
"Best luck on your opening night."

Poor Hamlet! It's fit to congeal ya,   *Ophelia*
To see what a hard fate can deal ya,
   For what did him in
   Was a prick in the skin,
When his prick should have been in Ophelia.

There was a young warrior of Parma   *Parma*
Who was having a medieval charmer.
   Said the madam, demure,
   "You'll excuse me, I'm sure,
But I wish you would take off your armor."[11]

It's sad to reflect on the past   *Past*
When one's tumescent reflex was fast;

---

[10] As a former history professor, I can only hope that Ned was chosen for his role in this limerick because his profession better satisfied the needs of the writer for an exact meter, and not because historians were prone to such activities.

[11] A sad fate pursued this young man from Parma. On another occasion he faced an equal admonition:

> There was a young fellow from Parma
> Who was solemnly screwing his charmer.
>   Said the damsel, demure,
>   "You'll excuse me, I'm sure,
> But I *must* say you fuck like a farmer."

Now one shouts, "Hip Hurray!"
If a half-hour's play
Can get the damn thing to half-mast.

Phyfe

There was an old burglar named Phyfe,
Who found burglaring the joy of his life.
When he entered a house
Through the bedroom, the louse
Scared the owner half out of his wife.

Plumbing

His Lordship was frenziedly plumbing
A bar maid whose pelvis was humming.
She exclaimed: "This is bliss.
He's come once doing this,
And we're close to the Lord's second coming."

Purdue

Said a passionate girl from Purdue
To her German professor Karl Schkrew,
"You think reading Nietsche
Is perfectly peachy,
But, frankly, I'd much rather screw."[12]

Rex

The play about Oedipus Rex
Has a plot that is very complex.
He clobbered his paw,
Then screwed his own maw,
While the chorus sang songs about sex.[13]

---

[12] She was obviously more experienced than her neighboring townsman:
> There was a young man from Purdue
> Who was only just learning to screw.
> But he hadn't the knack,
> He got too far back—
> The right church, so to speak, but wrong pew.

[13] The sad fate of mankind resulting from the inclinations of that early king has been memorialized in at least one other limerick:

A young Scottish soldier named Rex   *Rex*
Abstains from all manner of sex.
    He is more than a Spartan
    Because of his tartan—
He suffers from kiltie complex.

Said a young violinist from Rio   *Rio*
While seducing a girl named Cleo
    As she took down her panties,
    "Come now, no andantes,
Let's make this allegro con brio." [14]

A maestro directing in Rome   *Rome*
Had a quaint way of driving it home.
    Whoever he climbed
    Must keep her tail timed
To the beat of a loud metronome.

To probe Miss Lillian Russell   *Russell*
A friend thrust a pin in her bustle.
    He got a sprained wrist,
    And a mouthful of fist,
For the bustle turned out to be muscle. [15]

The king named Oedipus Rex,
Who started this fuss about sex,
    Put the world to great pains
    By the spots and the stains
Which he made on his mother's pubex.

[14] A well-known version pictures the lady musician in the limerick as somewhat more ambitious:

There was a soprano named Clio,
Who said to the boys in the trio,
    "When I take down my panties,
    Let's have no andantes—
Let's do it allegro con brio."

[15] The episode described in this tragic limerick may explain why Lillian Russell, a well-known turn-of-the-century singer and actress, at one time during her career sought an injunction restraining any manager from requiring her to appear in tights.

Sixty-nine
Three cheers for the year '69,
A year of erotic design.
　　It suggests a position
　　For oral coition,
Which suits nonvegetarians fine.[16]

Stead
For a phallus Miss Winifred Stead
Used a bar from the foot of her bed.
　　But lacking the touch
　　Of blacksmiths and such,
Kept her from forging ahead.

Stu
A short-peckered rabbi named Stu
Was vainly attempting to screw.
　　His wife said, "Oy veh!
　　You keep on this way
And the Messiah will come before you."

Sue
Said Jim to his big sister Sue:
"Ma's not as good fucking as you."
　　Replied Sue, tousjours gaie,
　　"That's what they all say—
Father, Uncle, and Grandpappy, too."

---

[16]The year 1969, with its reminder of the classical husband-wife (or man-woman) position, inspired a number of limericks. One of the best, certainly, is:
　　A newly wed husband named Bynham,
　　Asked his bride to please 69 him.
　　　　When she shook her head,
　　　　He sighed and then said,
　　"Well, if we can't lick 'em let's join 'em."
A venerable rhyme revived at that time recalled the origins of the practice:
　　Old Louis Quatorze was hot stuff.
　　He tired of a normal stuffed muff.
　　　　He upended his mistress,
　　　　Kissed hers while she kissed his,
　　And thus taught the world *soixante-neuf*.

Helen Keller's pussy grew tight,   *Tight*
As she rubbed her clit late at night.
   She tickled that gland
   With just her left hand
And silently moaned with her right.

A Nigerian lass, unprotected,   *Unprotected*
By a tiger was ate—and delected.
   The beast, though most hideous
   Was highly fastidious
(Her vulva was firmly rejected).

Where is the old-fashioned virtue?   *Virtue*
The values that will not desert you?
   Simple life, high resolve,
   Worthwhile problems to solve,
And a cozy vagina to spurt through?[17]

When at college a girl cannot win,   *Win*
What with studies and sex and bad gin.
   And it's just the last straw
   When the dean says, "Withdraw,"
When its him that's been sticking it in.

There was a young tutor quite wise   *Wise*
Who loved to feel cocks just for size.

[17] Any true limericist will recognize that the genius of this verse lies in the star-
tling contrast between the lofty, moralistic sentiment in the first four lines and the
earthy realism of the last. One version of a classic limerick illustrates the same point:
     There was a young girl from Aberystyth
     Thought safe with the man she played whist with,
       'Till one night they were found,
       Flat on the ground,
     Uniting the things that they pissed with.
Here the Victorian prudery, suggested by the game of whist, intensifies the shock of
the final revelation. So much for that lesson.

At every school dance,
He'd unzip the boys' pants.
They nicknamed him "Lord of the Flies."[18]

Yale   There was a professor at Yale,
Who searched for a fresh piece of tail.
He found in his class,
A quite young piece of ass.
Now he's spending his spare time in jail.[19]

Such a sampling, highly selective and reflecting my own tastes in limerickology, surely demonstrates the vast debt that all collectors owe the gifted members of the Society of the Fifth Line. Its seemingly inexhaustible additions to the world's supply of fresh materials have enriched and provided delight and inspiration to friends of this art form, wherever they may be. They have also greatly aided me in compiling this book. And so I can only show my appreciation by expressing my thanks in the traditional fashion:

[18] Here the play is upon the title of the popular novel published by William Golding, *The Lord of the Flies* (London and New York, 1954).

[19] Yale has long been a favorite of limerick writers; Gershon Legman's *The Limerick* lists no less than five honoring that institution, while Harvard warrants only three and Princeton none. This favoritism, I suspect, is due to the ease of rhyming "Yale" with "tail," rather than a judgment on the academic merits of those Ivy League institutions. Typical of the better-known verses using Yale as a setting is:

There was a young fellow from Yale
Whose face was exceedingly pale.
For while on vacation
He tried masturbation
Due to the high price of tail.

An old member with thoughts mercenary
Acquired the rights (literary),
    And published for you
    This brief *déjà vu*
Of a few from the Fifth Liner's library.

CHAPTER III

A Miscellany Principally Purloined

*A*ssembled in this chapter is a variety of limericks with no common theme, but essential to an appreciation of the literary variety and social impact of this unique verse form. Some few I have written, others have been provided by friends, still others have been culled from archival sources, but the majority have been plagiarized exactly or with slight variations from the several collections that have been printed over the years, most of them for private sale or in limited editions.

In selecting those for inclusion from the several thousand available I have used two criteria. One is the limerick's popularity, for many that deserve rank among the classics seem to be less well known than others, even though of comparable or superior merit. For some time I have tested acquaintances who profess to be expert collectors with these three, and a surprising number fail to pass:

> There was a young man from Cape Hatteras
> Who kept poking holes through the mattress.
>   He said with a wail,
>   "It's my wife's narrow tail.
> I'll have to get one with a fatter ass."

There was a young man from the war office,
Who went out one night with a whore of his;
    She took off her drawers
    In the manner of whores
But the man from war office tore off his.

    The Nobel prize for the immoral,
    The palm, the wreath, and the laurel,
        Goes to Josephine Buntz
        Who had three men at once,
    One fore, one aft, and one oral.[1]

Surely such gems deserve immortality. Inclusion in a book such as this may help restore them to the limelight that they deserve.

My second standard stems entirely from a personal prejudice. I am not in the least puritanical, not easily offended by any combination of four-letter words, not disturbed by the most eccentric exhibitions of sexuality. I do not, happily, qualify among the ranks of the saints, as does the hero of one limerick:

    In limericks I'm not a good trafficker,
    For my nature is much more seraphicker;
        My conscience sits queasily,
        I blush far too easily,
    And I do not collect pornographica.

---

[1] Talented as was Josephine Buntz, she was surpassed in sexual dexterity by another heroine:
    A whore had the idea sublime
    To take on seven men at a time:
        One on top, one beneath,
        In each hand, 'twixt the teeth,
    And two with her toes—for a dime.

But I do have a regrettable weakness: I simply do not like verses having to do with the excretion of bodily solids and fluids, either fore or aft. This, I hope, is a judgment that has nothing to do with morality or Freudian complexes. Some of my best friends are scatologists. By taste, however, I lean toward verses that glorify copulation, between male and female, male and male, female and female, male and animal, female and animal, and all the infinite variations thereof. These I have chosen for this anthology.

This does not mean that I have omitted all limericks that have to do with bodily functioning. Who could possibly exclude such a glorious example of the art as

> A Protestant lady named Alice
> Once peed in a Catholic chalice.
> "I do this," said she,
> "From a strong urge to pee,
> And not from sectarian malice."

Unfortunately those exploiting bodily functioning do not always conform to such high standards of delicacy.

Within the broad category that my prejudices dictate, I have tried to select limericks that are as subtle as the verse form allows. The very best, in my judgment, depend for their effect on the imagination (or depraved mind) of the reader, and not on the indiscriminate use of four-letter words. Few achieve the degree of perfection of:

> There was a young man from Dumfries,
> Who said to the girl on his knees,
> "You would heighten my bliss,
> If you played more with this,
> And paid less attention to these."

But others aspire, and those have been given preference on the pages that follow.

To select the few worthy of inclusion within the space limits prescribed for this volume has been a devastatingly painful experience. Classic after classic, favorite after favorite, has been relegated to the "discarded" file only after an agonizing struggle. What torture to cast aside the verse about the young man from Trent whose cock like a fishhook was bent, or those describing the exploits of the girl from Cape Cod who thought babies came from God, the old maid from Madras who had the most beautiful ass, the two young girls from Birmingham who lifted the frock of the bishop who was confirming them, the Argentine gaucho named Bruno who found llamas *numero uno,* the exotic miss from Chichester who made all the saints in their nitches stir, the nymphomaniacal Alice who used a dynamite stick for a phallus, the young widow from Ransom who was ravished three times in a hansom, the weary old lecher named Blot who took a luscious young blonde to his yacht, the talented miss from Detroit who at fucking was very adroit, the sad youth from Bengal who swore he had only one ball—and on and on and on. To omit each was to say farewell to a trusted friend of many years. I mourn them one and all.

The pages that follow would be far more appealing if all could be included. But most are in the standard collections, and all are in Gershon Legman's magnum opus, *The Limerick.* Those that have survived my tests will, I hope, provide learning and delight to those with tastes similar to my own.

There was a young man from Ann Arbor   *Ann Arbor*
Whose cock was cut off by a barber.
    In great consternation,
    He said, "Masturbation
Will henceforth be *very* much harder."

Befuddled by booze, Jacob Astor,   *Astor*
Tried to bugger a statue of plaster.
    Informed of his error,
    He recoiled in pure terror.
"Thank God," he said, "I am not faster."

A German musician named Bajer,   *Bajer*
Spurred on by a very high wager,
    Proceeded to fart
    The complete oboe part
Of a Haydn octet in A major.[2]

A virgin emerged from her bath   *Bath*
In a state of righteous wrath,
    For she'd been deflowered
    When she bent as she showered,
And the handle was right in the path.

There was a young lady from Bicester,   *Bicester*
Who said to the man who had kissed her,
    "Dear sir, you're uncouth—
    You have broken a tooth,
And left on my lip a large blister."

---

[2] An oboe-playing friend of mine tells me that this part probably consisted of:
"Beep, Beep, Boop."

Bicester

One day at a wedding in Bicester,
Said mama to the bride as she kissed her,
  "I think you'll have fun,
  With this boy you have won.
I did before tea, and so'd your sister."

Brighton

There was a young fellow from Brighton
Who thought he'd at last found a tight-un.
  He said, "Oh, my love,
  We fit like a glove."
Said she: "You're not in the right-un."[3]

Chaussey

A fellow who lived in Chaussey
Had a cock like the trunk of a tree.
  Said his wife, when in rut,
  "If it had but one nut,
'Twouldn't be such a chestnut to me."

Claire

A born-again Christian named Claire
Was having her first love affair.
  As she climbed into bed
  She reverently said,
"I wish to be opened with prayer."

Claridge

There was a young lady from Claridge
Who had a dress made for her marriage.

---

[3] The variety of the limerick maker's art is revealed by the many versions of this classic. Thus:

> There was a young sailor from Brighton
> Who remarked to his girl, "You're a tight 'un."
>   She replied, " 'Pon my soul,
>   You're in the wrong hole.
> There's plenty of room in the right one."

She said, "If you please,
Make it tight at the knees.
I won't have it done in the carriage."

Said Joan on the pile, "I confess,   *Confess*
To be burned at the stake is a mess.
Though I frankly avow,
I'm smoking more now,
But clearly enjoying it less.[4]

There was a young lady from Crewe   *Crewe*
Who said, "I don't drink, I don't chew.
But do not think, therefore,
There is nothing I care for,
If you get what I mean, and you do."

A penniless colleague named Cy,   *Cy*
Remarked to a lass passing by,
"I've never adjusted
To being flat busted."
Said she, with a sigh, "Nor have I."

There was a young fellow named Dan   *Dan*
Who was found jacking off in the can.
He said, "To be blunt,
It's less fun than a cunt,
But at least I'm a self-made man."

There was a young girl from Darjeeling   *Darjeeling*
Who danced with such exquisite feeling,

---

[4]This is one of several limericks built upon advertising slogans popular in the 1970s. One prominent cigarette manufacturer based a campaign on "Are you smoking more now and enjoying it less?"

Not a sound could be heard,
Not a murmur or word;
Only fly buttons hitting the ceiling.[5]

Daughter

There once was a clergyman's daughter
Who detested all boyfriends who sought her,
 'Til she found one whose dong
 Was as hard and as long
As the prayers her father had taught her.

Degeneracy

A young lady renowned for degeneracy
Told a friend if he wanted to have any, he
 Should lie in repose
 While tickling her toes
With his hand on her vaginal cavity.

Descartes

The eminent philosopher Descartes
Once let a considerable fart,
 But his mind couldn't tell
 If the fart had a smell,
Because body and mind are apart.

Dice

There was a young fellow named Dice
Who remarked, "They say bigamy's nice.
 Even two is a bore—
 I prefer three or four,
For the plural of spouse, it is spice."

---

[5] Ballet dancers seem destined to embarrassing situations in the hands of limerick writers. Thus:

 There was a young lady from Calais
 Who was cheered as she danced in the ballet.
  But the cheers turned to roars
  When she bursted her drawers
 And the hair on her head didn't tally.

They say a young fellow named Dutton *Dutton*
Had a penchant for all forms of mutton.
    Be it ewe, lamb, or ram,
    He gave not a damn,
But straightway began to unbutton.

A young man from upper East Lynn *East Lynn*
Had a penis quite short, limp, and thin.
    From whore after whore
    'Til he could take it no more,
He heard the sad words, "Is it in?"[6]

Said the queen to the Bishop of Ely *Ely*
As her quim he was starting to feely,
    "You no doubt are my sort
    For I've spied the great wart
On the end of your membrum virile."

Our cunning old grandmother Eva *Eva*
As adept with wit as with cleaver,
    When she saw Grandpa Adam
    And knew that he had 'em,
Made sure he would never deceive her.

One Japanese immigrant fears *Fears*
He's being deceived by his ears,
    When he hears from connections
    That we have our elections
Only once in evely four years.

[6] This short-peckered unfortunate was also embarrassed on his first date with a girl:

    There was a young fellow from Lynn
    Whose cock was the size of a pin.
        Said his girl, with a laugh,
        As she sought for his staff,
    "This won't be much of a sin."

Finnegan

A pious young lady named Finnegan,
Would caution a friend, "Now you're in again.
    Do time it right,
    Make it last through the night,
For I really don't want to sin again."

Found

An organic chemist soon found,
While pushing aminos around,
    He'd no sense of smell,
    And couldn't quite tell
His acids from holes in the ground.

Fyfe

A gentleman living in Fyfe
Made love to the corpse of his wife.
    "She was cold, didn't budge.
    So how could I tell, judge?
That's the same as she acted in life."[7]

Garden

Said a rose to a bee in a garden,
"Indeed, I do beg your pardon.
    But when you seek honey,
    It makes me feel funny.
I suspect you buzz in with a hard on."

Gladys

There was a young lady named Gladys,
Who instead of a dress wore a lattice.
    She said, "It is true,
    I provide a good view,
But why should you kick, ain't it gratis?"

[7] His experience was the opposite of the well-known widow:
    A young widow no man could entice,
    For she kept her dead husband on ice.
        "It's been hard since I lost him—
        I'll never defrost him.
    Cold comfort, but cheap at the price."

74

A rustic who lived in Gommecourt   *Gommecourt*
Went to Paris to visit a whore.
    He came back in a hack,
    Lying flat on his back.
"Did she burn you?" they asked. He said, "Shore."

    Of the mistress of W. Randolph Hearst   *Hearst*
    All friends suspected the worst,
        For over her bed
        Was the motto in red:
    "The Customer Always Comes First."

    There was a young girl with a hernia,   *Hernia*
    Who said to the doctor: "Gol dern ya,
        When you're slicing my middle,
        I pray do not fiddle
    With matters that do not concern ya."

    There was a young lady quite hot,   *Hot*
    Who inserted a fly in her twat.
        She did so becuz
        She imagined the buzz
    Was something she knew it was not.

    There was a young student named Jones   *Jones*
    Who'd reduce any maiden to moans
        Buy his wonderful knowledge,
        Acquired in college,
    Of nineteen erogenous zones.

There was a young lady from Kent   *Kent*
Whose cunt was so large in extent
    And so deep and so wide
    That accoustics inside
Were so good you could hear when you went.

Launcelot

There was a young fellow named Launcelot,
Whom his neighbors all looked on askance a lot.
    Whenever he'd pass
    A presentable lass,
The front of his pants would advance a lot.

Lynn

There was a young lady from Lynn
Who thought copulation a sin.
    But when her best beau,
    Tried to see if 'twere so,
She cried: "Please do it agin."[8]

McPherson

A happy old whore named McPherson
Was really the *busiest* person;
    Spent her nights, for a fact,
    In the sexual act
And all of her days in rehearsin'.

Madras

Well fucked was a boy from Madras,
By all of the lads in his class.
    Said he with a yawn,
    "Now the novelty's gone,
It is only a pain in the ass."

Madrid

There was an old whore from Madrid,
Whose usual price was a quid,
    But there came an Italian,
    With balls like a stallion.
He got it for nothing, he did.

[8]This young lady, obviously, was of different temperament from her Lynn neighbor:

> There was a young lady from Lynn
> Who thought fornication a sin.
>   But when she was tight,
>   It seemed quite all right.
> So everyone filled her with gin.

Said a Hollywood sex queen named Mae,   *Mae*
"I've returned from Hawaii to stay.
 The Islands are grand,
 But give me a land
Where a lay is a lay, not a lei."

When visiting a farmer, Mae West   *Mae West*
Lay down near a cow barn to rest.
 When she brushed a cow's udder,
 She would sleepily mutter,
"Just one at a time, boys, is best."

There was a young girl with hot meatus[9]   *Meatus*
Who engaged in frequent coitus,
 'Til an athlete from State
 Made her periods come late,
And now she has athlete's fetus.

A Far Eastern charmer named Ming   *Ming*
Liked to keep her beaux on a string.
 She wasn't a tease,
 But being Chinese
Was just an inscrutable thing.

An Englishman visiting Nahant   *Nahant*
Claimed nothing his courage could daunt.
 But after eight hours
 With a girl of vast powers
"Once more, dear," she asked. "No I cawn't."

A young lad from Eton named Ned   *Ned*
Wrote to his mother and said:

[9] A "meatus," believe it or not, is a bodily passage such as the opening of the ear or the urethral canal. Presumably it was not an inflammation of the ear that led to the embarrassing situation in which this young lady found herself.

"The headmaster here
Is a bit of a dear,
But must he spend nights in my bed?"

Northampton

A habit obscene and unsavory
Holds the mayor of Northampton in slavery.
With mellifluous howls
He deflowers young owls
That he keeps in an underground aviary.[10]

Norway

Quoth a comely young lady from Norway
As she hung by her heels in a doorway,
"Although I'm proficient
In arts concupiscent
Thank God, I've discovered one more way."[11]

Nothing

When college girls sit 'round doing nothing,
Their talk quickly turns to their rutting.
How pretend you're demure
When your crack's so mature,
That a man can fall through before coming.

---

[10] The buggery of owls has long been a favorite subject of limerick writers, probably because of the word's rhyming potential rather than the unique charm of that species. One typical example:
> The novelist, William Dean Howells,
> Kept a harem of deflowered owls,
> 'Till his parrot one day
> Phoned the S.P.C.A.,
> And complained of the state of their bowels.

Note, too, the unique charm of the word "mellifluous," rather than the usual "blood-curdling."

[11] Purists will note that the use of the one word "concupiscent" elevates this limerick from the ordinary to the sublime. The version found in most collections is:
> There was a young lady from Norway
> Who hung by her heels in a doorway.
> She said to her beau,
> "Look at me, Joe.
> I think I've discovered one more way."

"Madam," said Thomas O'Dore,   *O'Dore*
"I can't go on any more.
   I'm all in a sweat,
   And you haven't come yet,
And it's nearly a quarter past four."[12]

A tutor in German at Oriel   *Oriel*
Had a prick like the Martyr's Memorial.
   The display of this organ
   And the words "Guten Morgen"
Were the prelude to every tutorial.[13]

[12] This complaint of Thomas O'Dore is well known. Far less known is the answer that he received:

     "Tom," came a voice from the bed,
     "Such complaints are surely ill bred.
        Your pecker's so small,
        There's no friction at all
     To bring my desires to a head."

The limerick has also inspired a talented writer to shatter tradition by composing a more complex verse:

     "Dear wife," said Farmer O'Dore,
     "I think we should suffer no more.
     I've gone to great lengths
     And you've endured much pain,
     I've used all my strength
     And you've called sex a bane.
     So off to my cow, and you to your candle
     (By now you may need to use the axe handle).

[13] The Oxford colleges have inspired generations of limerick writers. This admirable verse is only one of several mentioning the Martyr's Memorial, an imposing shaft that stands in St. Giles, Oxford, at the head of the Cornmarket Street, as a memorial to Protestant martyrs killed during the reign of Queen Mary. Another that uses the same rhyme scheme but is less subtle:

     There was a young don from Oriel
     Who broke all rules proctorial.
        He walked down the Corn
        With a bloody big horn,
     And buggered the Martyr's Memorial.

Two other Oxford classics, among the many, are particularly worthy of a place in any anthology:

     The wife of a don of divinity
     For thirty years kept her virginity.

Oyster

A scandal involving an oyster
Sent the Countess of Clewes to a cloister.
    She preferred it in bed,
    To the Count, so she said,
Being longer, and stronger, and moister.

Pair

A happily married young pair
Were having a bout in a chair.
    On a powerful thrust
    The furniture bust,
But at that point they didn't much care.[14]

Plumber

There once was a lecherous plumber
Who boasted to every newcomer,
    How he went about smelling
    (I blush at the telling)
Girl's bicycle seats in the summer.

Port Said

There was an old whore from Port Said,
Who was found lying flat on a bed.

The boys up at Magdalen
Must have been dawdling.
It couldn't have happened at Trinity.

There was a young man from St. John's
Who started to bugger the swans.
    Said the loyal hall porter,
    "'Pray, sir, take my daughter.
The birds are reserved for the dons."

[14] The delightful last line of this verse contrasts markedly with the usual version:
There was a young man from Eau Claire
Who was having his girl in a chair.
    But the furniture broke
    On the thirty-fourth stroke,
And his gun went off in the air.
I must confess that this was the first limerick that I ever heard and include it for sentimental reasons. That I became addicted at this point is an obvious indication of my lack of taste.

(The obvious next line,
Is: Was she supine?)
"I'm not prone to argue," she said.[15]

There was an old fellow of Queens *Queens*
Who chased young girls in their teens.
 The number he raped,
 Minus those who escaped,
Was daily displayed on the screens.

There was a young lady of Rheims *Rheims*
Who amazingly pissed in four streams.
 A Doc, poking 'round
 A fly button found
Wedged tightly in one of the seams.

There was a young girl at the Ritz *Ritz*
Who loved men to nibble her tits,
 'Til a skilled Fletcherizer
 Made her sadder but wiser
By chewing them gently to bits.[16]

"My troops," Teddy Roosevelt said, *Said*
"Find Cuba is sexually dead,
 For the whores, whites and blacks,

---

[15] An alternate version, less instructional because it pays less attention to the grammatical differences between "prone" and "supine" is:
 A groom on the night they were wed
 Found his wife lying nude on the bed.
  "Why, darling, what goes on?
  You've not any clothes on."
 "I'm not prone to argue," she said.

[16] The world, alas, has forgotten Horace Fletcher, a nutritional expert at the turn of the century who advised eating in moderation and chewing food so thoroughly that it "swallowed itself." The words "Fletcherism" and "Fletcherize" were seen by a generation as synonymous with good health.

Will not risk their backs,
By taking Rough Riders to bed."[17]

Said

A professor of history once said,
"I enjoy two young girls in my bed.
One's black and one's white
But I swear in the night,
You can't tell the difference," he said.

Scout

There once was a little Girl Scout
Who found herself troubled by doubt.
"If that's only a finger,"
She said, "it may linger,
But otherwise take it right out."

Sholes

There was an old lecher named Sholes
Who longed to deflower young moles.
Although he aspired,
He was always too tired
After digging them out of their holes.[18]

Sicily

There was a young fellow from Sicily,
Whose tool was long, thick, and bristly.
'Twas a cock at whose sight
Women screamed with delight
But to tell you the truth, he fucked prissily.

---

[17] Time now for another history lesson. The "Rough Riders," a colorful regiment of volunteers recruited by Theodore Roosevelt at the outbreak of the Spanish-American War, consisted of western cowboys, eastern polo players, and a sprinkling of unsavory characters. They gained more publicity than territory, particularly when they were forced to leave their horses in the United States and fight on foot.

[18] His experience differed from that of a certain young lady:
There was a young lady from Coldsville
Who by chance sat down on a mole's hill
When a very young mole
Mistook hers for his hole.
The lady's all right, but the mole's ill.

When a budding philosopher went slumming   *Slumming*
He said to the girl he was plumbing,
   "According to Aquinas,
   My mind must be minus—
It's going, I fear, but I'm coming."

There was a young student at Smith   *Smith*
Who declared all virtue a myth.
   "For try as I can,
   I can't find a man
It is fun to be virtuous with."

Said a virgin librarian, Ms. Snook,   *Snook*
Who had learned about sex from a book,
   "No one at my age
   Should be harmed by a page."
But one tore off a piece, and it took.

There was a young girl named Sophia   *Sophia*
Who succumbed to her lover's desire.
   She said: "It's a sin.
   But now that it's in,
Could you shove it a few inches higher?"

Said Queen Isabella of Spain,   *Spain*
"I like it just now and again.
   But please let me explain,
   That by now and again
I mean *now* and again and again."

An eager young virgin named Mag   *Squat tag*
Thought all forms of sex were her bag.
   "An asparagus bed,"

She repeatedly said,
"Is a jolly good spot for squat tag."[19]

Sucker

Her husband's a chronic pipe sucker,
With teeth clenched on stem, lips a-pucker.
    But while he cogitates
    His poor wife masturbates.
What else, if you've got a nonfucker?

Surry

There was a young lady from Surry
Whose cunny was lusciously furry.
    It looked like a sort
    Of Viennese torte,
But it tasted like nine-week-old curry.

Swarthmore

A distinguished professor at Swarthmore
Propositioned a sexy young sophomore.
    As quick as a glance,
    He tore off his pants,
But he found that the sophomore'd got off more.

Sydney

There was a young lady from Sydney
Who could take it right up to her kidney.
    But a man from Quebec
    Put it up to her neck.
My, he had a big one, didn't he?

[19]The use of vegetables as phallic substitutes is well known among limerick makers. Thus:

> There was a young lady named Hatch
> Who sat down in a vegetable patch.
>   She said with a smile,
>   "I shall sit here awhile.
> There's a cucumber stuck in my snatch."

Said a madam with nice legal tact,   *Tact*
"It's a jurisdictional fact,
    My procedural duties
    Are managing young cuties
Without getting into the act."

She believed when he heatedly said   *Tail light*
That he loved her, and wanted to wed.
    She shortly got wise
    That the light in his eyes
Wasn't love light, but tail light instead.

There was a young lady of taste   *Taste*
Who was very well formed to the waist.
    So she limited love
    To the regions above,
And thus was eternally chaste.

A bitter new widow, quite tough,   *Tough*
To her mate's ashes said, in a huff,
    "You've diddled young girls,
    Never bought me no pearls,
And wanted me to blow you—so puff."

Said an ardent young bridegroom named Trask,   *Trask*
"I will grant any boon that you ask."
    Said his bride: "Fuck me, dearie,
    Until I grow weary."
He died of old age at the task.

An ambitious young harlot from Trier   *Trier*
Was eager to advance her career.
    Her boyfriend said: "Mabel,

Get off the damned table.
That buck is for the next beer."[20]

University
An instructor at Yale University
Fell on days of deepest adversity.
So he offered his ass
For the use of his class
In a classical form of perversity.

Utrecht
There was a musician from Utrecht
Whose organ was rusty and blue-specked.
Because of the cold,
It started to mold,
So his fuguing, un-Bached, became Brubecked.

Verdun
A skinny old maid from Verdun
Wed a short-peckered son of a gun.
She said: "I don't care
If there isn't much there.
God knows it is better than none."[21]

Wadham
There once was a warden of Wadham
Who approved of the folkways of Sodom.

[20] An alternate version is somewhat less to the point:
There was a young girl from St. Cyr
Whose reflex sensations were queer.
Her escort said, "Mabel,
Do get off the table;
The money's to pay for the beer."

[21] Her poorly endowed husband may well have been the hero of another verse:
Said a modest young man from French Lick,
"I confess that all girls make me sick,
For in North Carolina,
The smallest vagina
Is inches too large for my prick."

"For a man might," he said,
"Have a very poor head,
But be a fine fellow at bottom."[22]

There was a young lady from Warsaw   *Warsaw*
Who cared more for her trousseau than torso.
    But her impatient mate
    Was too eager to wait,
And that's why her trousseau was tore so.

Said a whore who lived wisely and well,   *Well*
"As for me, they can all go to hell.
    No man is exempted;
    They choose to be tempted.
Can I help if they buy what I sell?"

The Bishop of Bath and of Wells   *Wells*
Was deficient in spermatoid cells.
    His frail masculinity
    Explains the virginity
Of all the diocesan belles.

There was a young lady from Wheeling   *Wheeling*
Who professed to lack sexual feeling.
    But a cynic named Boris
    Just touched her clitoris,
And she had to be scraped from the ceiling.

---

[22] The warden would clearly have enjoyed meeting one of his Oxford contemporaries:

> There was a young fellow from King's
> Who was weary of women and things.
>   Said he, "My desire
>   Is a boy from the choir
> With an ass that's like jelly on springs."

Wimbley

A wanton young lady from Wimbley,
Reproached for not acting quite primly,
    Answered: "Heavens above,
    I know sex isn't love,
But it's such an attractive facsimile."

Yorick

A Shakespearean actor named Yorick
Was able in moments euphoric
    To bring to perfection
    Three kids of erection:
Corinthian, Ionic, and Doric.

Zoo

All the lady gnus at the zoo,
Were charmed by a young male gnu.
    The old bull was distressed
    To be thus dispossessed
By the tricks that the new gnu knew.

The Limerick and Today's World

*T*hroughout the ages, poets have been particularly sensitive to the events and moods of their day. They have recorded, in sonnet and ballad and ionic couplet, the wonders that they have seen, but they have captured also the underlying spirit that makes those events understandable to later generations. Their soaring stanzas bring home to us the genesis and meaning of the Age of Rationalism or the Age of Romanticism as could no other writing.

Who today could understand the multifaceted appeal of seventeenth-century American Puritanism without contrasting the gloomy stanzas of Michael Wiggleworth's "Day of Doom" with the passionate verses of Anne Bradstreet as she sang of the glories of her Creator. To Wigglesworth, and to many Puritans, the Deity was a heartless tyrant who took pleasure in condemning all sinners to eternal fire, even newborn babes who died before they had sinned:

> A crime it is, therefore in Bliss,
>   you may not hope to dwell,
> But unto you I shall allow,
>   the easiest room in hell.

To Anne Bradstreet the Creator was a kindly God, worthy of the glorification that inspired her poems:

What God is like to Him I serve,
What Savior is like to mine?
O, never let me from thee swerve
For truly I am thine.

Each of these poets revealed an aspect of a powerful religious impulse, no matter how different the nature of its appeal.

And so throughout the course of America's history. The patriotic fervor bred of the Revolutionary years was captured for eternity in the stirring stanzas of Philip Freneau:

Bend to the stars that flaming rise,
In western, not in eastern, skies,
Fair Freedom's reign restored.

The relentless impulse that drove men westward as they peopled the continent was made clearer when Walt Whitman sang:

All the past we leave behind.
We debauch upon a newer mightier world,
varied world,
Fresh and strong the world we seize, world of
labor and the march,
Pioneers! O pioneers!

Throughout mankind's intellectual adventuring, the poet has recorded and understood.

Nor have the geniuses who today produce the endless procession of limericks shirked their duty. They have sought to interpret and perpetuate the world in which we live today, and to explore the changes that the modern mood has wrought. A liberal sampling of the five-liners that fall into this category has been assembled on the pages that follow. These poems deal with a variety of topics: public morals, modern styles, mechanical inventions, transplants, the space age, women's struggle for equality, the awesome problems engendered by computers, and many more. All have in common a perceptive sensitivity to the problems of the current generation, and all will contribute to the understanding of those problems by future historians.

A scientist from Russia named Adam   *Adam*
Took a pot shot at splitting the atom.
    He blew off his penis,
    And now, just between us,
Is known in the Kremlin as Madam.

The eminent Christiaan Barnard   *Barnard*
Has labeled a baseless carnard
    That by using epoxy
    He can assure the cocks he
Transplants will always stay hard.[1]

[1] Limerick writers have long experimented with adhesives to provide variations in the sexual act. Two examples will suffice:

> There was an old harlot named Sue
> Who filled her vagina with glue.
>   She said with a grin,
>   "They paid to get in.
> Now they'll pay to get out again, too."

> There was a young couple named Kelly
> Who now live belly to belly.
>   One night in their haste
>   They used library paste
> Instead of petroleum jelly.

The eminent surgeon, Christiaan Barnard, gained fame for his pioneering work in heart transplants.

Beard
We men who develop a beard
Find it not as bad as we feared.
　　Though some babes do not care
　　For an excess of hair,
To stout pricks they all are endeared.[2]

Bed
A well-known psychiatrist said,
"We find sex to be all in the head."
　　Said his patient, "If true,
　　Will we hereafter screw,
In the library rather than in bed?"[3]

Black
A young lady scientist, Ms. Black,
Tried to mate with a large UNIVAC.
　　This gigantic computer
　　Proved itself neuter
By counting the hairs 'round her crack.[4]

Child
The sex I was taught as a child
I am told by my son is most mild.

---

[2] Probably so, but some women found that the "pricks" from the beards of their lovers caused problems:
　　A young bride was once heard to say,
　　"Oh, dear, I am wearing away.
　　　　The insides of my thighs
　　　　Just look like mince pies,
　　For my husband won't shave every day."

[3] For the less pure of mind, the final three lines of this limerick might be changed to:
　　Said Linda Lovelace,
　　"It's a far better place
　　To be screwed in the throat, not in bed."
Probably no limericist needs to be reminded that Linda Lovelace was the star in the X-rated film *Deep Throat,* which concerned the amorous adventures of an unfortunate young miss whose clitoris was in her neck.

[4] So rapid has been the development of the computer that few of us today can remember the boxcar-size monster known as the Universal Automatic Computer, or UNIVAC, that was in use only a generation ago.

His grammar school features
Exposure by teachers
And orgies at lunch that are wild.[5]

The new women's styles are first-class   *Class*
For revealing a shapely young lass.
　　But though better to view her,
　　It's tougher to screw her,
With her stockings up over her ass.

When the race to the moon runs its course,   *Course*
And women are sent there by force,
　　Will the men they embrace
　　In the vast outer space
Start to call making love "outercourse"?[6]

"If I kiss with my lips wide apart   *Dear Abby*
When dating my teen-age sweetheart
　　Will I get a baby?"
　　Dear Abby said, "Maybe,
But at least you'll have made a good start."[7]

A reader who writes from afar   *Dear Abby*
Asks if earrings the male image mar.
　　"I've worn them with pride

---

[5] This and several other limericks in this chapter are borrowed from the publications of the Society of the Fifth Line. That the members of this eminent society should pay such devoted attention to modern problems illustrates my point that poets are particularly sensitive to the moods of their day.

[6] I have also leaned heavily on *Playboy's Book of Limericks* in preparing this chapter on the modern scene. In doing so I pay tribute to its editor, Clifford M. Crist, an old friend and fellow member of the Society of the Fifth Line. His knowledge of the lore of the limerick is unsurpassed, and his own creations models of brilliant versifying.

[7] This limerick and the two that follow are based on actual letters that appeared recently in the syndicated advice column "Dear Abby." Authors of this form of verse are encouraged to read that column for inspiration as well as moral uplift.

Since my jealous young bride
Found one on the seat of my car."

Dear Abby

"Our problem is mutual orgasm—
I come before he has his spasm.
What shall I do?"
Dear Abby said, "You
Ought to take a large tuck in your chasm."

Disgrace

See-through fashions are such a disgrace,
We no longer remember a face;
Boobies in large batches,
And half-concealed snatches.
Imagining's quite out of place.

Dodge

A cautious young fellow named Lodge,
Had seat belts installed in his Dodge.
When his date was strapped in
He committed a sin
Without even leaving the garage.

Dosset

A linguistic purist from Dosset
Said: "Oh, dear, how long ago was it
That a person could say
That a party was gay,
And the gays were still locked in the closet?"

Dot

Said an activist female named Dot
"There's one thing I protesteth not,
When I lie in the street,
I think it real neat
To be carried off showing my twat."

Said a wise old fellow named Dunn,   *Dunn*
"I have heard that jogging is fun.
    But those of my age
    Will agree with the sage
Who said women and cows shouldn't run."

An X-rated movie emporium   *Emporium*
Is not just a super sensorium,
    But a highly effectual
    Heterosexual
Mutual masturbatorium.

There was a young physicist, Fiske,   *Fiske*
Whose art was exceedingly brisk.
    So fast was his action,
    That lorentz's contraction
Changed his tool from a rod to a disk.[8]

Said a potentate gross and despotic,   *Ford*
"My tastes are more cheap than exotic.
    I've always adored
    To make love to a Ford,
Because I am auto-erotic."

Despite Betty Friedan's fierce cry,   *Friedan*
There are some rights we men must deny.
    I think you'll allow, sirs,
    That feminine trousers
Need not be equipped with a fly.[9]

[8] As everyone knows, lorentz's reaction, a rule in modern physics stemming from Einstein's theories, holds that an object in rapid motion contracts.

[9] Betty Friedan, the militant writer and speaker on women's rights, is alleged to have called her mailman a "person person," and of making her defeated adversaries cry "aunt."

Friedan

The trouble with Betty Friedan
Is she misses the whole point of man.
    When Great God made the penis
    He was thinking of Venus;
Betty thinks of a trip to the can.[10]

Hatch

There was a young lady named Hatch
Who had a rectangular snatch.
    So she practiced coition
    With a mathematician
Who had a square root to match.[11]

Hatch

There was a young fellow named Hatch
Who thought he had made a great catch.
    His inducement to flirt
    Was a wee mini-skirt.
But alas, she had a huge maxi-snatch.

Kay

Ephraim and crusading Kay,
Love to picket by night and by day.
    They walk the same line
    And hold up a sign
Which shows where you see Eph you see Kay.

---

[10] Betty Friedan has, inevitably, inspired poets in many forms, most of whom seem to be unblushingly chauvinistic. Thus:
Betty Friedan
Would,
Stand at the can like a man,
If she could.

[11] He was more fortunate than another hero who suffered a dismal fate:
At last when his moaning was stifled,
He groaned: "I would never have trifled
    With Hortense the whore
    And gotten so sore
If I'd known her vagina was rifled."

"I have," said a girl in Khartoum,   *Khartoum*
"Been blocked by the man in the moon."
    But an astronaut's cock,
    It was rogered her twat,
And blasted off there much too soon.[12]

A transplant surgeon from Kelf   *Kelf*
Gave a girl's heart to an elf.
    He gave a marine
    Her liver and spleen,
But the best part he kept for himself.

Now that women have found liberation,   *Liberation*
They feel that male sex they can ration.
    So who do I turn to
    When I have the yearn to?
Thank God, there is still masturbation.

An unfortunate man from Madrid   *Madrid*
Had both superego and id.
    So whether he screwed
    Or entirely eschewed,
He suffered, whatever he did.

There was an old whore named Mallot   *Mallot*
Who bosted a gigantic twat.

---

[12] The impact of the modern explosion in scientific knowledge, as well as the improvement in limerick writing, is revealed by comparison with an earlier version involving this same young lady:
> There was a young girl from Khartoum
> Who was blocked by the man in the moon.
>   "It has been great fun,"
>   She remarked when he'd done,
> "But I'm sorry you came quite so soon."

No pecker could suit her,
But a large Roto-rooter
Would bring on the pleasure she sought.

Mate   Said a groom to his amorous mate,
"My dear, I'm afraid you must wait
For whatever comes next
I must study the text—
It's continued on page ninety-eight."

May   "Bee's knees" would cry dear old Aunt May,
"Cat's pajamas," my father did say,
I said "a cock-sucker,"
My son "Mother fucker"—
We've progressed a very long way.

May   A young airline stewardess, May,
Has achieved the ultimate lay.
She was screwed without quittin'
From New York to Britain.
It is clear that she's come a long way.[13]

Miss   Once bedded, a militant miss
Reacted to an amorous kiss,
"By God, all us sisters
Would kick out you misters
If we didn't need *that* to fit *this*."

Mission   A woman's lib gal with a mission
Explained her distaste for coition:

[13] This verse admirably illustrates the alertness of limerick writers to today's world. The line "It is clear that she's come a long way" were based on a slogan used by a popular cigarette in its advertising, assuring women that they'd "come a long way" along the path to equality.

> "Though fucking I love
> If I'm on him above,
> But I can't stand the lower position."

Those women who call themselves MS.,   *MS.*
Assert the perogatives of HS.
    Though clearly obsequious
    In matters quite devious
They still want to sit down to PS.[14]

With new morality sweeping the nation   *Nation*
And the candor of sex information,
    They've relocated sex
    Deep down in girl's necks.
I ask you, is *this* masturbation?[15]

The U.N. at last reached N.Y.C.   *N.Y.C.*
Though most wished it in nearby CT.
    But a delegate shouted,
    "Decency would be flouted
If you put the U.N. in CT."[16]

---

[14] Alternate versions that exploit the same theme are understandably numerous. Two indicate the possibilities:

> The gains now achieved by a MS.
> Make her world more equal to HS.
>   But parity dangles
>   By reason of angles,
> For the MS. lacked the standing to PS.

> Here's to the girls known as MS.
> They've usurped a world once HS.
>   They've taken our clothes,
>   Our jobs, and our beaux,
> But they still have to sit down to PS.

[15] Those sufficiently curious to penetrate the meaning of this timely verse should consult footnote 3 in this chapter and there learn about the book and film called *Deep Throat.*

[16] I am proud to say that this gem was written especially for this book by America's leading limericist, Clifford M. Christ, who has aided immeasurably in all aspects of its compilation.

Occidental

On a flight with a young occidental,
I tried to be specially gentle.
  She was so delighted
  That we flew United,
Though we were aboard Continental.

Peeping Tom

When they finally caught "Peeping Tom" Moyer,
Long thought a campus-cop voyeur,
  The A.C.L.U.
  Got him out of his stew.
"An invasion of privates," said the lawyer.

Physician

A classic case for a physician
Is a matron who tried each position,
  And nothing would suit her
  Until a computer
Prescribed her appendix incision.

Pill

A government file clerk named Jill
Has now started taking the pill.
  It's not for enjoyment
  But because her employment
Depends on it, up on the Hill.

Pox

Said an anxious young lady named Cox,
"I on birth control pills wish a pox.
  Some find them divine,
  But when I try mine
They always fall out of my box."

Psychoanalysis

The people who live in large palaces
Set no store in psychoanalysis.
  When you talk about Freud,

They are bored and annoyed
And cling to their long-standing phalluses.[17]

A man, although young, begins to fear he's   *Queries*
As dated as last year's world series,
    When the *Post* and the *Times*
    Proclaim in headlines,
HOMOSEXUAL WEDDINGS RAISE QUERIES.

Said an eager young surgeon from Souling,   *Souling*
"So far we have only been fooling,
    But it soon won't vex us
    To change both the sexes.
It's only a case of retooling."

A physicist miss in Milnocket   *Rocket*
Used for solace a solid-fuel rocket,
    But the heat of her quim
    Ignited the rim.
Now she's worn by her beau in a locket.

The right to decide how to screw   *Screw*
Is one that all femmes now pursue.
    If the girls get their voice
    In making a choice,
It won't be "how," but will be "who."

[17] Sigmund Freud and his theories have been justly immortalized in many limericks. Thus:

> The late psychoanalyst, Freud,
> Was at normalcy greatly annoyed.
>   But bugger your brother
>   Or knock up your mother,
> He was—page after page—overjoyed.

Stutz

A women's lib leader named Stutz
Is known to have plenty of guts.
　　When asked what she'd need
　　To be totally freed,
She snarled at her questioner, "Nuts."

Transplants

In these days of sexual transplants
A guy really takes quite a chance.
　　Are the charms of this muff
　　The original stuff,
Or are they from one of his aunts?

Venus

There was a young spaceman from Venus
Who had a prodigious penis.
　　Cried his girlfriend, "Alas,
　　It just came out of my ass,
And there's still fifteen inches between us."

Viable

Since transplants have proved to be viable
And my dong's becoming less pliable,
　　Why not graft as a ringer
　　My trusty third finger,
Which today is much more reliable.

Whippersnapper

There once was a young whippersnapper
Whose ways were so pristine and dapper,
　　That a young lady's quim
　　Held no interest for him
If it hadn't a cellophane wrapper.

Bibliography

Index

Bibliography

In compiling this bibliography I have had the invaluable aid of Clifford M. Crist, that master of the medium who compiled the Playboy's Book of Limericks. This listing contains most modern works on the subject including what we hope is a complete catalogue of the publications of the Society of the Fifth Line.

Aiken, Conrad. *A Seizure of Limericks.* New York, 1963. Fifty original limericks, all of them, alas, clean.

The Archives. Cambridge, Mass., n.d. A collection of earthy verses and tales gathered by a "Gentleman about Town" and published by his Harvard friends after his untimely death in a plane accident. Limericks, all of them well-known classics, are on pp. 5–16.

Asimov, Isaac. *Lecherous Limericks.* New York, 1975. A popular volume containing one hundred original limericks, many of them superb examples of the medium.

Asimov, Isaac, and Ciardi, John. *Limericks: Too Gross.* New York: Norton, 1978. An excellent collection of original limericks, many of them destined to become classics.

Baring-Gould, William S., ed. *The Lure of the Limerick: An Uninhibited History.* New York, 1967; London, 1968. A fine introduction on the history of the limerick, followed by a first-rate collection of limericks, most of them classics.

The Bawd's Book: Being a Collection of Crass and Curious Limericks and Linoleum Cuts. San Marino, Calif. 1965. A dozen classics, illustrated and printed in a small edition.

Crist, Clifford M., ed. *Playboy's Book of Limericks*. Chicago, 1972. A splendid collection of original and classical limericks, many written by the editor, assembled from the files of *Playboy Magazine* or reprinted from publications of the Society of the Fifth Line.

Douglas, Norman. *Some Limericks*. Florence, 1928, and many subsequent editions. Notable for the hilarious footnotes written by Douglas.

————. *Some Limericks*. New York, 1964. A paperback collection, *Le Ballet des Muses*.

Hart, Harold D., ed. *Immortalia—Volume I: Limericks*. New York, 1970. Originally published in Philadelphia in 1927 in a small, privately printed edition for subscribers. It contains the usual well-known classics.

Legman, Gershon, ed. *The Limerick: 1700 Examples with Notes, Variants and Index*. Paris, 1953; later editions New York, 1964, 1969. A bible of all limerick collectors, with scholarly variant readings, an excellent historical introduction, a thorough index, and an amazingly complete collection of limericks, arranged by topic.

————. *The New Limerick*. New York, 1977. An additional 2,750 limericks that did not appear in *The Limerick*. This is another superb collection arranged by topics, with a forward, bibliography, notes, and variants, and a complete bibliography.

The Limerick: A Facet of Our Culture. Mexico City, 1944. The usual collection of 276 well-known limericks, with a good historical introduction.

Noble, Fillmore P. [Albin Chaplin]. *The Noble Five Hundred Limericks*. New York, 1967. Five hundred limericks, all of them written by the author.

————. *The Limerick That Has the Appeal*. Detroit, 1976. Over two thousand limericks, topically arranged. Most of the five hundred in his prior book are reprinted here.

Pepys, J. Beauregard [Roy W. West]. *Limericks for the Main Line, or*

The Art of Social Descending Made Easy. Philadelphia, 1973. Sixty original limericks focused on the Philadelphia scene.

――――. *The Lilt of the Tilt, or The Flasher in the Rye.* Lahaska, Pa., 1978. Limericks in Scottish dialect.

Society of the Fifth Line. *Source Material Group I.* Chicago, 1954. A mimeographed collection of limericks contributed by members at the first meeting of the Society of the Fifth Line. An excellent index is included.

――――. *Source Material Group II.* Chicago, [1955]. Mimeographed. A smaller collection of materials, apparently gathered at the second meeting of the society.

――――. *Where the Scatological Is the Necessary: A Prolegomena to the Poetics of the Limerick.* Chicago, 1958. The first Norman Douglas Memorial Lecture, delivered at the Society of the Fifth Line at the Union League Club of Chicago on 13 May 1957.

――――. *The Limerick in the Nuclear Age: The Second Annual Norman Douglas Memorial Lecture Delivered to the Society of the Fifth Line May 9, 1958, at the Union League Club of Chicago, Illinois.* [Chicago 1959.] Mimeographed and bound. Contains also: "Annotation Presented to the Society of the Fifth Line, May 9, 1958, by the Secretary Pro Tem."

――――. *The Limerick and the Other Arts: A Study in Cross-Fertilization.* Chicago, [1960]. The third Norman Douglas Memorial Lecture, delivered to the society at the Union League Club of Chicago on 8 May 1959.

――――. *Little Known Limericks of Ella Wheeler Wilcox.* [Chicago, 1961.] *The fourth Norman Douglas Memorial Lecture, delivered to the society on 13 May 1960 at the Union League Club of Chicago.*

――――. *North against South: A Centennial Appraisal.* Chicago, [1962]. The fifth Norman Douglas Memorial Lecture, delivered to the society on 12 May 1961 at the Union League Club of Chicago.

――――. *The Gray Flannel Limerick, or Friendly Persuasion through the Ages.* Chicago, [1963]. The sixth Norman Douglas Memorial

Lecture, delivered to the society on 9 May 1962 at the Union League Club of Chicago.

———. *Venus Looks at the Earth's Genitalia, or Cox and Box.* Chicago, [1964]. The seventh Norman Douglas Memorial Lecture delivered to the society on 10 May 1963 at the Union League Club of Chicago.

———. *Ontogeny Recapitulates Phylogeny?* Chicago, 1965. The eighth Norman Douglas Memorial Lecture, delivered to the society on 8 May 1964 at the Union League Club of Chicago.

———. *Proceedings of the Annual Meeting of the Society of the Fifth Line, 1965.* Chicago, [1965]. Contains "Minutes of the Thirty-first Annual Meeting" of the society held on 8 May 1964 at the Union League Club of Chicago, a "Letter from the Top of the Ivory Tower," a "Report on Limericks in Mexico," and "The Society Work Project, 1965."

———. *The Seventy-fourth Annual Meeting of the Society of the Fifth Line, May 14, 1965.* Chicago, [1966]. Minutes of the meeting of the society held on 14 May 1965 at the Union League Club of Chicago, a "Scientific Commentary," and a "Society Work Project."

———. *The Curious Case of the Crypto-Limerick.* Chicago, [1966]. The ninth Norman Douglas Memorial Lecture, delivered to the society on 14 May 1965 at the Union League Club of Chicago.

———. *The Five Lines of Force of Gall and Spurzheim.* Chicago, [1967]. The tenth Norman Douglas Memorial Lecture, delivered at the "seventy-fifth anniversary celebration" of the society on 13 May 1966 at the Union League Club of Chicago.

———. *Seventy-sixth Annual Meeting of the Society of the Fifty Line, May 12, 1967.* Chicago, [1967]. Minutes of the annual meeting of the society held on 13 May 1966 at the Union League Club of Chicago, together with limericks presented at the 1967 meeting.

———. *Limericks of the Transplant and Other Things: Seventy-seventh*

Annual Meeting of the Society of the Fifth Line May 10, 1968.
Chicago, [1968]. Contains minutes of the meeting of the so-
ciety on 12 May 1967, held at the Union League Club of Chi-
cago, as well as sections on "Hands across the Sea" and "Lim-
ericks of the Transplant and Other Things."

———. *Miracle of Majorca.* Chicago, [1968]. The eleventh Nor-
man Douglas Memorial Lecture, delivered on "the seventy-
seventh anniversary of the Society of the Fifth Line," 12 May
1967, at the Union League Club of Chicago.

———. *Transplants: The Twelfth Norman Douglas Lecture, Delivered
on the Seventy-eighth Anniversary of the Society of the Fifth Line,
May 10, 1968, Union League Club of Chicago.* Chicago, [1969].

———. *Proceedings of the Seventy-eighth Annual Meeting of the Society
of the Fifth Line, May 8, 1969.* Chicago, [1969]. Contains min-
utes of the annual meeting of the society held at the Union
League Club of Chicago on 10 May 1968, and the thirteenth
Norman Douglas Memorial Lecture, "True Confessions and
Dying Warnings in Colonial New England," delivered before
the society on 8 May 1969 at the Union League Club of Chi-
cago.

———. *The Society of the Fifth Line, 1970.* Chicago, [1970]. Con-
tains minutes of the "seventy-eighth annual meeting of the
society," 9 May 1969, at the Union League Club of Chicago,
the fourteenth Norman Douglas Memorial Lecture—"When
Knighthood Was Deflowered"—delivered on 8 May 1970 at
the Union League Club of Chicago, and "Limericks of
Women's Liberation and Other Things."

———. *Proceedings of the Eighty-first Annual Meeting of the Society of
the Fifth Line, May 14, 1971.* Chicago, [1971]. Contains min-
utes of the "seventy-ninth annual meeting" held on 8 May
1970 at the Union League Club of Chicago, a "Report of the
Women's Liberation Committee," the fourteenth [*sic*] Nor-
man Douglas Memorial Lecture on "Groping in the Secret
Drawers of Publishing," delivered on 14 May 1971 at the

Union League Club of Chicago, and three collections of limericks: "Report of the Fifth Line Chartered World Tour," "Minorities," and "New Material."

―――. *Society of the Fifth Line, 1972: Minutes, 1971, of the Society of the Fifth Line.* Chicago, [1972]. Contains minutes of the meeting of 14 May 1971 at the Union League Club of Chicago, the fifteenth Norman Douglas Memorial Lecture on "Making It Hard for Pornographers," and three collections of limericks headed "New Material," "Unlikely Candidates," and "Consumer Protection."

―――. *Proceedings of the Eighty-third Annual Meeting, Society of the Fifth Line.* Chicago, [1973]. Contains minutes of the meeting held on 12 May 1972 at the Union League Club of Chicago, the sixteenth Norman Douglas Memorial Lecture on "The Fifth Line and the Fifth Column," and three collections of limericks: "Sex Education," "Women's Lib," and "New Material."

―――.*Society of the Fifth Line.* Chicago [1974]. Contains minutes of the 1973 meeting, the Norman Douglas Memorial Lecture on "I'd Rather Be Naked than Dead, or The Monroe Doctrine," and collections of limericks on "Exorcism," "Inflation," "The Energy Crisis," and "New Material."

―――. *Society of the Fifth Line.* Chicago, [1975]. Minutes of the meeting held in May, 1974, the Norman Douglas Memorial Lecture on "The Double Helix—a Geneticist Looks at the Limerick," and three sections on limericks: "Spontaneous Limerick Exercises," "Colonial and Revolutionary Poems," and "New Material."

―――. *Society of the Fifth Line.* Chicago, [1976]. Contains minutes of the meeting held at the Union League Club of Chicago in May, 1975, the Norman Douglas Memorial Lecture on "The Bawdic Revival, with Special Reference to the Cinquain in Anapestic and Iambic Trimeter and Dimeter As a Reflection of Contemporary Sexual Mores," and four collections of limericks on "The Presidential Handicap," "New Material," "Bicentennial Philosophy," and "Impromptu Limerick Competition."

———. *Society of the Fifth Line.* Chicago, [1977]. Minutes of the society meeting held at the Union League Club of Chicago in May, 1976, the Norman Douglas Memorial Lecture on "Please Pass the Salt," and limericks dealing with "Sensitive Payments," Mechanical Alarm Devices," "Self Help," "New Material," and "Limerick Competition."

———. *Minutes of the Annual Meeting of the Society of the Fifth Line, 1977.* Chicago, [1978]. Contains minutes of the annual meeting held on 6 May 1977 at the Union League Club of Chicago, the Norman Douglas Memorial Lecture on "Is the Neo-Scatological Necessary?" and two sections of limericks: "New Material" and "Competition."

To Solace the Blind. Universitäts-Buchhandlung, Frankfurt am Rhein, 1945. Contains a section on "The Gardener's Tool" and 144 limericks, many of them original. A very rare book, of which only one copy is known. Most of the original limericks have been reprinted in Crist, *op. cit.*

Index

Screwing (*continued*)

> bison, 31; by northern Cheyenne Indian, 32; failure of cowboy to, 32; of dry wells by Texan, 33; of whore from Des Moines, 33; by cowboys in Dodge City, 33; inability to of Wild Bill Hickok, 34; viewed with alarm in Kansas, 35; of Mrs. Simpson by Edward, 42; by men of ETUSA, 42; by WACS, 42; of Madam Lupescu, 43; of USO hostess, 45; by amorous abbot, 50; of opera singer, 50–51; attempt to by sextagenarian, 51; refusal to by ballerina, 52; used to revive model, 53; of model by Titian, 53; preparing for with cork, 54; in bed of Sweet William, 55; of virgin named McNary, 55; of young lady from Maine, 55; of Little Nellie, 56; by William Vaughan Moody, 56; in medieval armor, 57; desired by student of German, 58; by Oedipus Rex, 58; to beat of metronome, 59; attempted by rabbi, 60; of Sue, 60; approval of, 67; of bridegroom, 70; refusal to in carriage, 71; of wife's corpse, 74; skills of learned from book, 75; enjoyed by McPherson, 76; worn out by, 77, 79; in chair, 80; prissily by man from Sicily, 82; desired by queen of Spain, 83; leads to death of Trask, 85; prescribed by computer, 92; in outer space, 93; in Dodge car, 94; of girl with rectangular snatch, 96; by astronauts, 97; by a Roto-rooter, 98; of airline stewardess, 98; use of textbook in, 98; decision on how to, 101

Seattle, girl from ravaged by cattle, 38
Second Coming, anticipated by Lordship, 58
Sexual activity, pleasures of, 20–101; variant activities of, 20–101
Sexual intercourse, *see* Screwing
Shale, effects of diddling with, 35
Sicily, well-hung man from, 82
Sioux Indians, who did nothing but screw, 28; screwing of by Colonel George A. Custer, 32; before attack on Custer, 33; well-hung young, 39; old squaw from, 39
Sitzkrieg, lack of praise for, 44
Sixty-nine, as position to please vegetarians, 60
Smith College, girl at declares virtue a myth, 83
Snatches, *see* Vaginas
Snook, Ms., harmed by a page, 83
Sodomy, *see* Buggery
Soixante-neuf, *see* Sixty-nine
Sophia, asks to have it up higher, 83
Souling, transplant surgeon from, 101
Sousa, John Philip, screwing to tunes of, 42